PENGUIN WRITERS' GUIDES

How to Punctuate

George Davidson is a former senior editor with Chambers Harrap. In addition to writing dictionaries and thesauruses, he is the author of several books on English grammar, usage, spelling and vocabulary. He lives in Edinburgh.

D0715365

The Penguin Writers' Guides

How to Punctuate   *George Davidson*
How to Write Better English   *Robert Allen*
How to Write Effective Emails   *R. L. Trask*
Improve Your Spelling   *George Davidson*
Writing for Business   *Chris Shevlin*

PENGUIN WRITERS' GUIDES

How to Punctuate

GEORGE DAVIDSON

PENGUIN BOOKS

PENGUIN BOOKS

Published by the Penguin Group
Penguin Books Ltd, 80 Strand, London WC2R 0RL, England
Penguin Group (USA) Inc., 375 Hudson Street, New York, New York 10014, USA
Penguin Group (Canada), 10 Alcorn Avenue, Toronto, Ontario, Canada M4V 3B2
(a division of Pearson Penguin Canada Inc.)
Penguin Ireland, 25 St Stephen's Green, Dublin 2, Ireland
(a division of Penguin Books Ltd)
Penguin Group (Australia), 250 Camberwell Road,
Camberwell, Victoria 3124, Australia (a division of Pearson Australia Group Pty Ltd)
Penguin Books India Pvt Ltd, 11 Community Centre,
Panchsheel Park, New Delhi – 110 017, India
Penguin Group (NZ), cnr Airborne and Rosedale Roads, Albany,
Auckland 1310, New Zealand (a division of Pearson New Zealand Ltd)
Penguin Books (South Africa) (Pty) Ltd, 24 Sturdee Avenue,
Rosebank 2196, South Africa

Penguin Books Ltd, Registered Offices: 80 Strand, London WC2R 0RL, England

www.penguin.com

First published 2005
1

Set in 11/13 pt Adobe Minion
Typeset by Rowland Phototypesetting Ltd, Bury St Edmunds, Suffolk
Printed in England by Clays Ltd, St Ives plc

ISBN-13: 978-0-141-02159-1

www.greenpenguin.co.uk

Penguin Books is committed to a sustainable future
for our business, our readers and our planet.
The book in your hands is made from paper
certified by the Forest Stewardship Council.

Contents

Introduction   vii

1   What is punctuation *for*?   1

2   Good and bad punctuation – and how to
improve yours   13

3   Sentences and non-sentences   23

4   Full stops   42

5   Question marks   56

6   Exclamation marks   68

7   Commas   77

8   Semicolons   130

9   Colons   140

10   Dashes   155

11   Quotation marks   168

12   Brackets   184

13   Ellipsis   191

14   Obliques   196

15   Apostrophes   199

16   Hyphens   209

17   Capital letters   231

18   Paragraphs   250

19   Italics, boldface type and underlining   252

20 Direct speech, correspondence, and essays
and reports   257

Technical terms   272

Bibliography   278

Index   281

Introduction

*the Nowing ones complane of my book the fust edition
had no stops I put in A nuf here and thay may peper
and solt it as they plese*

Timothy Dexter, *A Pickle for the Knowing Ones*

Timothy Dexter was an eccentric 18th-century American merchant who wrote a short book entitled *A Pickle for the Knowing Ones*. Among the notable features of this book were its bizarre spelling and the fact that it had not a single 'stop' or punctuation mark in it. When people complained that the lack of punctuation made the book difficult to read, Dexter published a second edition which included all the punctuation he considered necessary – four pages of punctuation marks placed at the end of the book, with an invitation to readers to 'pepper and salt' the text with them as they pleased.

Many people today are so baffled by punctuation that they would find great relief in dealing with the problem in much the same way as Timothy Dexter did, by doing away with punctuation altogether in their own writing and leaving it up to others to do the punctuating for themselves. If you are looking at this book, it may be that you are one of these people. Full stops, commas, colons and semicolons – you are never quite sure which to choose and where to put them.

Of course, omitting all the punctuation marks in

your letters, memos, essays and reports is neither a sensible nor a realistic solution to your problem. Punctuation is not some optional extra in a piece of writing, to be added in if one chooses, but is an integral part of what is written. Jonathan Swift, the author of *Gulliver's Travels*, once defined good style in writing as 'proper words in proper places'. One could well expand his definition a little, however, and say that good writing involves 'proper words in proper places, properly punctuated'. To write well, you must not only choose your words carefully, spell them correctly and arrange them grammatically; what you write must also be punctuated appropriately.

The problems entailed in choosing the right words, spelling them correctly and forming them into grammatical sentences are beyond the scope of this book, but if punctuating sentences appropriately is your problem, *How to Punctuate* can certainly help you. If you find punctuation difficult, it may be because you have never been taught it at all or because you have not been taught it properly. In either case, this book is the answer to your problem. Chapter by chapter, the correct uses (and also many of the wrong uses!) of each of the punctuation marks are explained, with examples of both correct and incorrect practice. As you work your way through the book, *your punctuation will improve*, and by the time you have reached the end of the book, you will be able to punctuate correctly and confidently. You need never fear being let down by your punctuation again.

You may, of course, not want to work through this book systematically from beginning to end, and you do not need to. *How to Punctuate* is equally suitable for systematic study, for casual browsing or for quickly checking particular points you are not sure about. By consulting the index at the back of the book, you can quickly and easily home in on any aspect or detail of punctuation you want to check.

You may have noticed that this is quite a long book, longer than many other books on punctuation available in bookshops. Do not be put off by this. Many punctuation guides give broad outlines of the main punctuation rules but do not deal in sufficient detail with specific problems. *How to Punctuate* provides more advice and the answers to more problems than many other books, while its clear and straightforward structure and full index make it easy to consult.

Contents

A key feature of *How to Punctuate* is its emphasis on the *sentence* as the basic unit of punctuation. Most punctuation guides do not stress this point sufficiently. Unless you are clear about what is, and what is not, a sentence, you cannot hope to punctuate any piece of writing correctly. Chapter 3 therefore deals in some detail with sentences and non-sentences. The contents of this chapter are of fundamental importance in punctuation and should be studied carefully by anyone who wants to improve their punctuation.

Chapters 4 to 14 deal with each of the punctuation marks in turn, showing how they are correctly used (and often how they are misused). The implications of different punctuation marks are explained by means of similar but differently punctuated examples. (The same point may be explained in more than one chapter, so all the necessary information is where you need it without your having to flick from chapter to chapter.)

Punctuation does not, of course, consist only of full stops, commas, colons, dashes, and so on, but also includes apostrophes, hyphens and capital letters. The correct use of these is dealt with in Chapters 15 to 17.

Good paragraphing and text layout, while perhaps not actually punctuation, have an important role in the conveying of meaning to a reader by making texts more readable. These topics are dealt with briefly in Chapter 18. Chapter 19 explains the uses of underlining, italics and boldface type.

Finally, Chapter 20 is devoted to the correct punctuation of direct speech; letters and addresses; bibliographies, references and footnotes; and quotations.

This book assumes no prior knowledge in the reader (apart from a basic knowledge of English). It is therefore suitable for native speakers and learners alike. Technical terms have been kept to a minimum, but they have not been avoided altogether as they are useful labels that assist explanations. All technical terms are fully explained in an appendix at the end of the book.

The variety of English described in this book is British English. American English differs from British English in many respects (in punctuation as well as in vocabulary, spelling and grammar), and the main punctuation differences between these two major forms of English are described at various points throughout the book.

Examples

How to Punctuate includes examples of both correct and incorrect punctuation. Examples of incorrect punctuation are always marked with the symbol ✗. The symbol ☒ is used when the punctuation is suspect but not definitely wrong. Examples of good punctuation are generally unmarked, but the symbol ✓ is used occasionally to draw attention to correct punctuation.

Acknowledgements

All the writers whose books are listed in the bibliography (page 278) have contributed in some way to the writing of this book, even where I have disagreed with their recommendations.

I would also like to thank Mark Handsley for his helpful comments on an earlier draft of this book.

1
What is punctuation *for*?

The writer who neglects punctuation, or mispunctuates, is liable to be misunderstood.

Edgar Allan Poe

These words of Edgar Allan Poe, the 19th-century American poet and short-story writer, encapsulate perfectly the purpose of punctuation and the dangers that lie in not taking punctuation seriously enough: when you write, you punctuate your sentences in order to help other people read and understand what you have written, and if you punctuate carelessly, what you have written may not be understood or, perhaps even worse, may be misunderstood.

Speech and writing

But why *is* punctuation so important to understanding a piece of writing?

Although they both serve to convey information from one person to another, speech and writing differ in several respects. It is precisely because of these differences that punctuation is needed and has been developed and refined over the centuries.

Speech consists of much more than just the words we speak, the sounds of which can be adequately represented in writing by the letters of the alphabet. There are also various vocal and non-vocal devices that we use in speech to make our meaning clear: intonation, rhythm, pauses, loudness, facial expressions, gestures, and so on. All these help to gather words into sense groups and to convey certain aspects of meaning that the words alone might not convey. When we write, none of these mechanisms are available to us, and so we use punctuation to convey both the structure of the text and the various nuances of meaning that the different vocal and visual devices would convey when we speak. Say the following four sentences out loud to yourself and consider the ways in which the punctuation marks and capital letters indicate differences in pronunciation that convey important differences in meaning and emphasis:

He's not coming.
He's not coming?
He's NOT coming?
He's not coming!

Furthermore, when we are speaking to someone, it is usually in a face-to-face – or at least voice-to-voice – context. We are therefore able to pick up and immediately correct any misunderstandings that arise. This is not possible with a written text, because the writer is usually not present when the reader is reading what has been written. It is therefore important that writers use every means available to them to make their meaning absolutely clear and prevent misunderstandings arising in the first place, because they will not be there to explain to their readers what they *really* meant if the readers get the wrong end of the stick.

One of the means available to writers for this purpose is punctuation, and that is why punctuating correctly is every bit as important as choosing words carefully and writing grammatically.

The recent history of punctuation

Of course, the system of punctuation that we have today did not come into existence all at one time. Compared to writing, punctuation is a relatively recent invention. While writing developed from drawing during the fourth century BC in Sumer in Mesopotamia (modern Iraq), even the simplest forms of punctuation did not come into use until some time later. There is no need in this book to cover the history and development of punctuation over the centuries, but it is worth noting that the conventional system of punctuation symbols that we use today developed very gradually, only fully coming into effect about the 16th century.

Punctuation has continued to change and develop since that time, and is still doing so. Some of these developments are worth mentioning here.

From rhythm to grammar

Until the end of the Middle Ages, punctuation was used to mark the *speech rhythms* of a text rather than its grammatical structure. Punctuation marks were provided as a guide to reading a text aloud or chanting it in church, and therefore it marked, for example, where to take a breath, where to pause, and how long to pause for. From the 16th century onwards, however, punctuation was increasingly used to clarify the *grammatical structure* and the *meaning* of a text rather than its rhythmic structure.

Nevertheless, the use of punctuation to mark pauses in a text continued beyond the 16th century, and indeed is still a feature of present-day punctuation. For example, as will be seen in Chapter 7, a comma may be inserted into a sentence at a point where the writer wishes to mark a pause, and sometimes (as will be seen in the discussion on page 120) the pauses do not correspond exactly to the grammatical structure of the sentence. So although grammar and logic have replaced rhythm as the main factors underpinning good punctuation, the rhythms of speech cannot be ignored entirely.

From heavy to light punctuation

We use far fewer punctuation marks per sentence now than was normal in even the recent past. This is due to a great extent to a change in our style of writing. In the past, good writers writing formal literature tended to use longer sentences than is now normal, and this naturally required more punctuation to break up the sentences and guide readers through their structure.

With the current trend towards shorter and simpler sentences, far fewer punctuation marks are required in the average sentence.

How punctuation works

Mr Speaker, I said the honourable member was a liar it is true and I am sorry for it. The honourable member may place the punctuation where he pleases.

Richard Sheridan, the playwright and politician, on being ordered to apologize for calling a fellow MP a liar

Punctuation clarifies writing by giving the reader information that the letters of the alphabet alone cannot do. As can be seen from the supposed 'apology' from Richard Sheridan, a sentence without punctuation can often be read in more than one way. (Try it for yourself. Put a comma after 'liar' and another one after 'true' and read the sentence. Then put a full stop after 'liar', a capital *I* at 'it', and keep the comma after 'true', and see what difference this punctuation makes to the sense of what Sheridan said. Which version is actually an apology?)

It may be helpful, before we go any further, to have a more detailed look at *how* punctuation clarifies writing. It does this in five ways: punctuation **separates words, groups words** and **links words**; it **differentiates between similar words and structures**; and it **represents emotional aspects of speech** in ways that the letters of the alphabet alone cannot do.

Punctuation separating and grouping words

When most people think of punctuation, what they usually have in mind is punctuation marks such as full stops and commas. But even the spaces between words on a page are a form of punctuation that makes texts easier to read. Consider the following passage from George Orwell's *Animal Farm*:

itwasabitterwinterthestormyweatherwasfollowedbysleetandsno wandthenbyahardfrostwhichdidnotbreaktillwellintofebruarythe animalscarriedonasbestastheycouldwiththerebuildingofthewin dmillwellknowingthattheoutsideworldwaswatchingthemandtha ttheenvioushumanbeingswouldrejoiceandtriumphifthemillwasn otfinishedontime

It is, of course, possible to read this passage as it stands, even if you have to do so very slowly and from time to time have to correct misinterpretations of what you are reading. But how much easier it is to read the passage when spaces separate the words, full stops and capital letters mark off sentences, and commas separate parts of sentences:

It was a bitter winter. The stormy weather was followed by sleet and snow, and then by a hard frost which did not break till well into February. The animals carried on as best as they could with the rebuilding of the windmill, well knowing that the outside world was watching them and that the envious human beings would rejoice and triumph if the mill was not finished on time.

In a more complex passage, the need for punctuation marks becomes even more obvious:

*Ourleadercomradenapoleonannouncedsquealerspeakingveryslo
wlyandfirmlyhasstatedcategoricallycategoricallycomradesthats
nowballwasjonessagentfromtheverybeginningyesandfromlongb
eforetherebellionwaseverthoughtof*

It might take you several attempts before the structure of this passage became entirely clear. On the other hand, once the punctuation is added, it is perfectly straightforward:

'Our leader, Comrade Napoleon,' announced Squealer, speaking very slowly and firmly, 'has stated categorically – categorically, comrades – that Snowball was Jones's agent from the very beginning – yes, and from long before the Rebellion was ever thought of.'

As you can see from these two passages, at the same time as separating words from each other punctuation also forms them into groups and marks off these groups. Once a passage of writing is punctuated, a reader can immediately see which words belong together and which do not. It is hardly surprising that Timothy Dexter's readers (see page vii) complained about the lack of punctuation in his book.

The above examples show how punctuation, by grouping words, makes passages of writing easier to read and understand. But that is not the only result. By separating words into groups, punctuation also brings out differences in meaning. Look at the following pairs of examples and see how the presence or absence of commas, or the position of the commas, affects their meaning (and notice also that the commas generally correspond to slight pauses in the sentences as they would be spoken):

The girls wanted to stay till Julian arrived. (because they liked Julian)
The girls wanted to stay, till Julian arrived. (because they didn't like Julian)

John said his sister was already married. (the sister was married)
John, said his sister, was already married. (John was married)

Mary went topless on one occasion only, because there were other women there who were topless. (stresses it was only on one occasion)
Mary went topless on one occasion, only because there were other women there who were topless. (stresses it was because there were other topless women there)

Other activities were arranged for the boys, who were too young to go sailing. (that is, for all the boys, because they were all too young to go sailing)
Other activities were arranged for the boys who were too young to go sailing. (that is, only for some of the boys, because they were too young to go sailing)

They had left thankfully. (they were thankful)
They had left, thankfully. (I was thankful)

Punctuation linking words

The main form of word-linking punctuation is hyphenation. Hyphens show that two or more words in a text are to be taken together as a single unit of meaning.

Consider this sentence from a news report:

Thousands of illegal migrants make the perilous voyage each year, often in rickety ships run by people smuggling rings.

Why, you might ask, do people who are smuggling rings take illegal migrants along as well? It must increase the likelihood of their getting caught. A hyphen in *people-smuggling* would, of course, make it clear that these two words are acting as a single unit in the sentence and that what is meant is that the ships are run by gangs of people-smugglers, not ring-smugglers. The hyphen makes the intended sense clear, while the absence of the hyphen suggests a totally different and incorrect interpretation of the sentence.

A hyphen may sometimes be in contrast with a comma. Consider the difference between the following pairs of examples:

the deep-blue sea (sea that is deep blue in colour)
the deep, blue sea (sea that is both deep and blue)

a light-green dress (a dress that is light green in colour)
a light, green dress (a dress that is both light and green)

The linking hyphens and the separating commas give entirely different meanings to the phrases.

Punctuation differentiating words

Look at this sentence from a newspaper report:

There have been attempts to rob postmen and women of Giro cheques.

Who exactly were the victims of the attempted robberies? According to the sentence as it stands, the attacks had been made on postmen and on women.

However, in the context of the whole report, it is clear that the attacks were being made on postmen and postwomen.

How could the writer of the report have shown that what was meant was not *all* women but just post-women? By means of a hyphen:

There have been attempts to rob postmen and -women of Giro cheques.

This use of the hyphen is frequently neglected. Another option would, of course, have been to spell out 'post-women' in full:

There have been attempts to rob postmen and postwomen of Giro cheques.

Hyphens are not the only form of punctuation used to distinguish words consisting of the same letters. Apostrophes also have this function. Notice the difference the position of the apostrophe makes in these examples:

the boy's boots (one boy)
the boys' boots (more than one boy)

The writer George Bernard Shaw was an ardent proponent of spelling reform. Among his *bêtes noires* were apostrophes, which he called 'uncouth bacilli'. In his own writing, Shaw regularly omitted apostrophes, writing *dont, havnt, shant, shouldnt* and *wont* instead of *don't, haven't, shan't, shouldn't* and *won't*. However, even he apparently drew the line at omitting the apostrophe from *he'll*. The following examples show why:

*John says the boys may want to go swimming tomorrow. He'll
take them if they do.*
*John says the boys may want to go swimming tomorrow. Hell
take them if they do.*

Punctuation representing emotion and attitude

Question marks and exclamation marks are used to
indicate that sentences are not statements, and capital
letters are used to indicate loudness or an emphatic
tone of voice. Compare the following examples:

That isn't true.
That isn't true?
That ISN'T true?
That isn't true!
THAT isn't true!

A change of typeface or underlining can be used for
the same purpose:

That isn't *true.*
That isn't true.

Hyphens can also be used to indicate particular quali-
ties of speech, such as hesitation or uncertainty:

Ye-es. I suppose that's possible.
We-e-ell. Maybe you're right, but I don't think so.

Quotation marks can be used to add a particular nuance
to what is being said. Compare the following examples:

Sheridan worded his apology very carefully. (he apologized)
Sheridan worded his 'apology' very carefully. (he didn't really
apologize)

In speech, what is implied by the quotation marks round 'apology' would be indicated by a combination of pausing, stress and intonation.

What we have had here is just a brief overview of the main functions of punctuation, illustrated with examples of only a few punctuation marks and techniques. There will, of course, be many more examples in the chapters that follow. But if you have now grasped the main uses of punctuation, you are well on the way to improving your own punctuation, which is the subject of the next chapter.

Summary of key points

- Punctuation clarifies writing by giving the reader information that the letters of the alphabet alone cannot do.
- Punctuation separates, groups and links words, so clarifying the structure and meaning of a piece of writing.
- Punctuation differentiates words that would otherwise be identical.
- Punctuation indicates emotion and attitude.

2

Good and bad punctuation – and how to improve yours

. . . most people would probably agree that punctuation is a matter not only of rules but of personal taste.

G V Carey, *Mind the Stop*

Taste and commonsense are more important than any rules; you put in stops to help your reader to understand you, not to please grammarians.

Sir Ernest Gowers, *Plain Words*

What is 'good punctuation'?

There are at least two answers to the question, 'What is good punctuation?' If you have read the Introduction to this book and Chapter 1, you will already be aware of one of them:

Good punctuation is punctuation that clarifies a piece of writing and makes it easier to read and understand.

This is essentially what Gowers means when he says that you put in stops (that is, punctuation marks) to help your reader to understand you rather than to please grammarians. Punctuation has the practical aim of making writing easier to read and understand, and that is as important as adhering to any rules.

But perhaps Gowers goes too far in saying that taste and common sense are *more* important than rules in punctuation. There *are* rules of punctuation and anyone who wants to punctuate well must learn them and obey them. So a second answer to 'What is good punctuation?' would be:

Good punctuation is punctuation that obeys the current established rules.

To paraphrase Carey, good punctuation is a matter *not only* of personal taste *but also* of rules. You can, of course, decide not to punctuate sentences with capital letters and full stops, but if you do, you will be breaking two of the fixed rules of English punctuation. The use of full stops and capital letters are established rules of English punctuation, and they must be adhered to.

Note the word 'current' in the second rule above. Like every other aspect of language – spelling, pronunciation, vocabulary and grammar – punctuation has changed over the years and continues to change. Today's punctuation norms are not the same as those of a hundred years ago, 50 years ago, or even 20 years ago. Norms change . . . but at any given time there *are* still norms, a set of good practices which should be understood and adhered to.

Of course, because punctuation evolves, there are inevitably grey areas where there is disagreement among authorities over what is or is not to be considered good practice. Some authorities may be more conservative in their judgements and recommendations, while others may be more accepting of recent innovations and developments. It is, as Carey says, sometimes just a matter of personal taste. *How to Punctuate* tries to steer a sensible middle course through these difficult and sometimes muddy waters, neither clinging rigidly to the norms of the past nor welcoming uncritically all recent developments (some of which seem quite undesirable and to be based more on carelessness and ignorance than on sound judgement).

Rules and choice in punctuation

If there are rules of punctuation, whatever they may be at any given time, is there always just *one* correct way of punctuating a given sentence? No, not necessarily. Punctuation is an *art*, not a *science*, and as Gowers and Carey imply, knowing the rules is not enough: common sense, personal judgement and personal taste also have a part to play. (Carey suggests elsewhere in his book that punctuation is governed 'two-thirds by rule and one-third by personal taste'.)

It is, however, important to know and understand the rules properly before you begin to apply your own taste and judgement. While a sentence can often be punctuated correctly in more than one way, there may only be one correct way or one particularly appropriate way of doing so to convey a particular meaning. Before you make your own personal choices, you need to know and understand the options that are available to you and their implications.

Appropriate level of punctuation

Finally, two more things need to be said about good punctuation. Firstly, you need to choose an appropriate level of punctuation to suit your subject matter, your intended readers and your style of writing. For example, you are more likely to use colons and semicolons in formal writing than in informal letters and emails, as your sentences are likely to be longer when you are writing in a more formal style. But secondly, and on the other hand, you should as a general rule use no more punctuation than is required to do the job. The lighter your punctuation, the better: if you find that you are having to use heavy punctuation in your writing, you should consider simplifying, splitting or shortening your sentences.

Summary of key points

- You use punctuation to help your reader understand what you have written.
- To punctuate correctly, you must know and adhere to the current established punctuation rules.
- You should use no more punctuation than is absolutely necessary. Light punctuation is better than heavy punctuation.
- You should suit your punctuation to the style of what you are writing.
- While knowing the rules of punctuation is important, good punctuation requires a sensible and discerning approach to their application. Good punctuation requires thought and common sense.
- Good punctuation allows a certain amount of personal choice.

Nine key ways of improving your punctuation

1. Don't be afraid of punctuation

Good punctuation really isn't difficult to achieve. All it takes is the knowledge of a few rules (all fully explained in this book), the application of a few general principles, some common sense, and a bit of thought.

2. Get a firm grip on the rules and broad principles first

Common sense and personal taste may be important in punctuation, but the way to punctuate well is to learn the fundamentals first. You cannot make a sensible personal choice between, say, a comma and a semi-colon or between a semicolon and a full stop until you are absolutely clear about the principles involved and the implications of your choice.

3. Read actively

When you are reading, take time to look at the punctuation other people use in their writing, and ask yourself why they have chosen that punctuation and whether you agree with their choice.

Do not, however, copy other people's mistakes. If you see punctuation that is not what you would have expected, don't just assume that it is you who are wrong. Other people can make mistakes too. (Sadly, much of what you read nowadays may be badly punctuated.)

Also, do not forget that the rules of punctuation have changed over the years, and the punctuation you will find in older writers such as Charles Dickens or Jane Austen is not necessarily appropriate nowadays. Model yourself on good *modern* writers.

4. Make a punctuation book

Note examples of good punctuation in a notebook or computer file. Build up a file of examples of good practice. Along with the examples you put in your file, note the rules that apply.

If you find examples of bad punctuation in other people's writing – and you will – you could note them also, along with corrected versions and the rules that explain them.

5. Think carefully about what you are trying to say

To punctuate correctly, you must understand your own message. If *you* do not know exactly what you are trying to say, it is hardly likely that whatever punctuation you add to your writing will make your message any clearer. Punctuation is an aid to clarity of expression; it is in itself neither the source of, nor a substitute for, clarity of thought.

The benefit of clear thinking is that, when you have a clear idea of the message you are trying to convey and know the punctuation options and their implications, many punctuation problems solve themselves.

6. Keep your sentences short(ish)

The longer and more complicated your sentences, the more difficult it will be to punctuate them and the more likely you are to make mistakes. Of course, you don't want to have a text full of nothing but very short sentences; that would make what you have written rather boring. An interesting piece of writing will consist of a variety of sentence types and lengths. But the longer and more complicated a sentence, the more punctuation you will need, and the more room there is for error. In the early stages of improving your punctuation, make things easy for yourself. Don't be too ambitious. Avoid problems.

7. Change the text to make punctuation easier

Sometimes a punctuation problem can suggest a need to change the way something has been expressed. Look at the following passage adapted from a letter to a newspaper:

In response to Joyce Holloway's recent column, does she have elderly parents; does she have children; has she been divorced; has she been financially ruined; has she ever lost her job?

The correspondent has written a series of questions separated by semicolons, and rounded them off with a sole question mark at the end of the sentence. Is this correct? Should there be question marks at the end of every question? Should there then be capital letters at the beginning of every question? And in that case, should there be semicolons at all? The writer himself may have been unsure.

The source of this problem lies in the structure of the whole sentence. There is, strictly speaking, something missing, because the questions do not actually follow logically or grammatically from the part beginning 'In response to . . .'. They need to be introduced by something like 'I would like to ask . . .'. Adding this to the beginning of the sentence improves the sentence, and at the same time the punctuation becomes easier. This would be one solution:

In response to Joyce Holloway's recent column, I would like to ask her the following questions: Does she have elderly parents? Does she have children? Has she been divorced? Has she been financially ruined? Has she ever lost her job?

As a rule, if you find it difficult to punctuate something you have written, check to see whether it is the structure of your sentence that is causing the problem. If it is, recast the sentence and the punctuation problem may just go away. Write in such a way that you avoid problems and you will make fewer mistakes.

8. Check your work

When you have finished writing, always go over it carefully and ask yourself why you have put a full stop here, a comma there. Was it a deliberate choice, and was it the right choice? If you're not sure, stop, think, and if necessary check up in this book. This may be slow going at first but, as with any art, you will improve with practice. You will soon have the knowledge to make the right choice at the first attempt and will rarely have to make changes.

Know your weak points. Always look for mistakes you know you are liable to make. (It is a good idea to check your punctuation book or file from time to time in order to remind yourself of the errors you tend to make or have made in the past.)

Do not rely on the grammar and punctuation checker on your computer. They are not very reliable and the suggestions they make are often not at all helpful. Make your own choices, and know why you have made them. You don't need a punctuation checker, and of course it will often be the case that you haven't access to one (e.g. in an exam). But if you do feel you have to use your computer's punctuation checker from time to time, do so *actively*: don't just accept its suggestions – look at them carefully and decide for yourself whether you agree or not. And do check that your punctuation checker is set for *British* English, not American English. The rules are different.

Don't agonize over your choices. There are often two or more possibilities and little to choose between them. Have confidence in your decisions (once you have consulted this book and know the rules!). If you haven't broken any rules, and if what you have written is clear and there is nothing in it that would mislead the reader, then let it be. It's probably fine.

9. Practise

And lastly, practise. Practice does make perfect. No matter what you are writing, never say to yourself that the punctuation doesn't matter. Get into good habits. Avoid sloppy punctuation at all times. Punctuate informal emails and letters to family and friends as carefully as formal letters, reports, essays, and so on. Even if you use emoticons, or smileys, in emails, always try to fit standard punctuation in as well (see page 262).

One way of practising punctuation would be to study what comes through your letterbox. A great deal of the junk mail we all receive is very poorly punctuated (it has been a fruitful source of examples of bad punctuation for this book), and correcting it provides good practice in punctuation.

3
Sentences and non-sentences

'Begin at the beginning,' the King said, gravely, *'and go on till you come to the end; then stop.'*

Lewis Carroll, *Alice's Adventures in Wonderland*

But *where* to stop? That, for many people, is the problem. It is easy enough to *start* a sentence, but knowing where to *stop* is a bit trickier. How do you know you have written enough to make a complete sentence but not less than a sentence or more than a sentence? Faced with this problem, many people seem to simply scatter a random selection of full stops and commas over their writing and hope for the best. But clearly that won't do.

Sentences are the key units of language within which punctuation operates. If you are not clear about what is or is not a sentence, what the various types of sentence are, and what the various elements are that form a sentence, you will never be able to punctuate correctly.

But *don't panic*. While you need to know *something* about sentences in order to punctuate properly, you do *not* need to learn a lot of difficult grammar. Without involving very much grammar at all (though a few technical terms will be found to be helpful), this chapter will tell you all you need to know about sentences. You *don't* need to learn everything in it, but it will certainly help you punctuate correctly if you read through it carefully.

What is a sentence?

There have been many different definitions of a sentence (one book lists about two hundred), and quite frankly most of them are of little help to anyone who is struggling with punctuation. For example, many of us will have learned something like this at school:

A sentence begins with a capital letter and ends with a full stop, a question mark or an exclamation mark.

Now, this is a perfectly valid definition of a sentence, and if you apply it to any page in a book, magazine or newspaper, you will easily pick out all the sentences. But if you are trying to *write* sentences, it is no help at all. Where do you put a full stop? At the end of a sentence. How do you know you are at the end of a sentence? That's where the full stop is. It's completely circular.

Here is another, more promising, definition of a sentence:

A sentence expresses a complete thought.

But what is a 'complete thought'? Consider this sentence:

The boy was choking.

This sentence describes one action or situation, so arguably it is expressing one 'complete thought'. But now look at this sentence:

James dashed out into the garden, grabbed the boy and thumped him on the back.

Is that still a single 'complete thought'? If so, how about when the same event is described in two sentences? Look at the following example:

James dashed out into the garden. He grabbed the boy and thumped him on the back.

Clearly the 'complete thought' definition of a sentence, while an improvement on the 'capital letter to full stop' definition, does not take us far enough. But it is nevertheless worth keeping in mind when you are writing. If a sentence you have written seems to be rather on the long side, ask yourself how many separate 'thoughts' or ideas it encapsulates: perhaps you could, and should, split it into two or more shorter sentences.

Recognizing sentences by their structure

A third way of identifying sentences is by their *structure*. Once you can identify the various types of sentence and their basic parts, you will more easily recognize where one sentence should end and the next one begin and where you should put commas within sentences.

Sentences have many different structures and they cannot all be covered here. Fortunately, they can be dealt with in four broad categories: **simple sentences,** composite sentences, super-sentences, and **reduced sentences**. (This terminology is not that of traditional grammar, but it suits the purposes of this book.)

Simple sentences

The most basic type of sentence is the *simple sentence*.

• Structure

Simple sentences can be divided into two main parts: the **subject** and the **predicate**. The subject of the sentence is the person or thing being spoken about:

He read the letter with satisfaction.
Caroline had hardly slept that night.
The plane flew low over the hills.
James shook his head.
She was absolutely amazed.
Her father is a policeman.

The predicate is what makes up the rest of the sentence:

*He **read the letter with satisfaction**.*
*Caroline **had hardly slept that night**.*
*The plane **flew low over the hills**.*
*James **shook his head**.*
*She **was absolutely amazed**.*
*Her father **is a policeman**.*

The core of the predicate is always a **verb**. A verb usually describes the action or activity of the subject:

*He **read** the letter with satisfaction.*
*The plane **flew** low over the hills.*
*James **shook** his head.*

Notice that a verb may be separated into two parts by some other word:

*Caroline **had** hardly **slept** that night.*

The verb may have an **object**:

*He read **the letter** with satisfaction.*
*James shook **his head**.*

Some verbs do not have objects. There is no object in either of these sentences:

Caroline had hardly slept that night.
The plane flew low over the hills.

Sometimes a verb simply links the subject to what follows in the sentence, helping to describe the state or condition of the subject:

*She **was** absolutely amazed.*
*Her father **is** a policeman.*

The descriptive word or phrase that follows a linking verb is usually known as a **complement**:

*She was **absolutely amazed**.*
*Her father is **a policeman**.*

Complements are found after other verbs as well:

*He found the door **open** and the money **gone**.* (= 'the door was open and the money was gone')

Some predicates may also have **adverbs** or **adverbial phrases**, words that describe 'how', 'when', 'where', etc:

*He read the letter **with satisfaction**.*
*Caroline had **hardly** slept **that night**.*
*The plane flew **low over the hills**.*

Simple sentences may be expanded in various ways, for example by providing more information, adding people's names, or including comments:

Tom goes to the opera.→ Tom only goes to the opera to please his wife.
Where are you? → Where are you, George?
You must say nothing about this. → You must, for all our sakes, say nothing about this.

As can be seen from the first example, a simple sentence may contain more than one verb:

*Tom only **goes** to the opera to **please** his wife.*

A verb that follows 'to' (called an **infinitive**) does not count as a 'full' verb. Whatever its length or complexity, a simple sentence always contains only *one subject* and *one main verb* associated with the subject.

The subject of a simple sentence may include one or more linking words (and there may also be some commas):

***Neither** John **nor** I will be at the meeting.*
*Mary **and** Joseph arrived at the inn.*
*Peter, Paul **and** Mary were all at the party.*

The same is true for objects, complements and adverbs:

*She bought bread, milk, eggs **and** cheese.*
*We were poor **but** happy.*
*I'll be here next week **and** the week after.*

When *verbs* are linked in this way, the sentences are considered to be composite sentences (see below).

There are other elements that could be mentioned in the analysis of simple sentences, but for our purposes it is not necessary to go into greater detail. You should now be able to recognize a simple sentence when you see one or when you write one.

• Punctuation

Short simple sentences require very little punctuation. Often there is only a capital letter at the beginning of the sentence and a punctuation mark (full stop, question mark or exclamation mark) at the end:

The kitchen was empty.
Where have you put my slippers?
Run for it!

Longer simple sentences may require commas as well:

John, Paul, George and Ringo were in some pop group or other in the sixties.
Outside, in the garden, she told the detective her story all over again.
*One's gardening clothes are almost always worn, torn, patched, faded **and** stained.*

Composite sentences

• Structure

Simple sentences are the basic building-blocks of writing. While they often stand alone, they can also be linked in various ways to form longer sentences. When two or more simple sentences are linked in some way, they form **composite sentences**, and the simple sentences themselves are then referred to as **clauses**. Look at these examples:

The sun rose over the mountains. It painted them a brilliant orange. (two simple sentences)
The sun rose over the mountains and painted them a brilliant orange. (composite sentence)
As the sun rose over the mountains, it painted them a brilliant orange. (composite sentence)

The words that link clauses in a composite sentence are called **conjunctions**. Conjunctions are words like *and, or, but, although, because, as, since, when* and *unless*.

There are two types of clause: **main clauses** and **subordinate clauses**. The main clause is the clause that describes the main action or topic of a sentence:

*As the sun rose over the mountains, **it painted them a brilliant orange**.*
***I'll tell you** when I see you.*
***You can go** if you want to.*
***We didn't speak again** until we had finished our drinks.*
***He shrugged** as he reached for his car keys.*

Subordinate clauses often have the same function as adverbs, saying when, where, how, etc the action of the main clause happens:

***As the sun rose over the mountains**, it painted them a brilliant orange.*
*I'll tell you **when I see you**.*
*You can go **if you want to**.*

A subordinate clause may be the object of a verb:

*Tell me **what happened**.*
*I think **there has been an accident**.*
*She knew **she sounded like a schoolmistress**.*
***What he was doing there**, goodness only knows.*

. . . or the subject of a verb:

***What he does now** is of no concern to me.*

Some subordinate clauses have a descriptive function, like adjectives:

*Have you still got the book **that I lent you**?*
*His latest book, **which is about UFOs and crop circles**, was lying on the floor beside the bed.*

Two or more main clauses may be linked by words such as *and, or* or *but*. Main clauses linked in this way are 'equal partners' in the sentence; neither is subordinate to the other:

*He smiled sadly **and** turned away.*
*The sun was shining on the ski slope **but** it was still very cold.*
*He hadn't raised his voice, **but** his tone was quite definitely threatening.*
*We've got to act now **or** it will be too late.*
***Either** John will be at the meeting **or** I will.*

Composite sentences may comprise more than one main clause and subordinate clause. Look at the following examples (where // marks the breaks between clauses):

*I don't know // why he said // what he said // but I can
guess // that he was rather upset // because he thought // we
had let him down.*
*When she came out of the room, // she glanced up and down
the corridor // and decided // that it was safe to go on // so
long as the guards did not waken.*

The key feature of a composite sentence is that, no
matter how long it is, the clauses are usually linked by
means of conjunctions.

Some subordinate clauses do not actually have a
verb in them at all:

Once inside the building, *the thieves made straight for the
safe.*

There *could*, of course, be a subject and verb in the
clause:

*Once **they were** inside the building, the thieves made straight
for the safe.*

Another type of subordinate clause worth noting is
one in which there is a verb in the form of a **participle**
(a word ending in -*ing*, -*ed*, -*en*, etc) or an infinitive:

Feeling *rather tired after her long trip, she went straight to
bed.*
Shaken *by the storm, the old tree finally collapsed.*
To help us out, *John came round every evening after work.*

• **Punctuation**
When the clauses of a composite sentence are linked
by conjunctions, there is often no need for any punctuation between the clauses:

I'll tell you when I see you.
You can go if you want to.

However, it may be that not *all* the clauses are linked in by conjunctions: often, only the last two clauses of a composite sentence are linked in this way, in which case the others are simply separated by a comma:

*He took a pencil out of his pocket, picked up the notepad **and** begin to write.*

*The old man noticed the coin, bent down to pick it up, spat on it, rubbed it on his sleeve, slipped it into his pocket **and** hobbled on.*

Even with a conjunction, if a subordinate clause precedes the main clause, the two clauses will usually be separated by a comma as well:

Once they were inside the building, the thieves made straight for the safe.

Feeling rather tired after her long trip, she went straight to bed.

Super-sentences
• **Structure**

Super-sentences are like composite sentences in that they consist of more than one clause, but differ from them in that each of the separate parts of the sentence is itself a complete sentence (which itself may consist of one or more clauses). The separate parts are not linked by conjunctions (though they may contain conjunctions) but are separated by semicolons.

A couple of examples of super-sentences will clarify this explanation:

I didn't mention the risks her actions involved; I didn't fully realize them myself at the time.

We have a close relationship; he trusts my judgement; he takes my advice.

This use of the semicolon will be discussed in more detail in Chapter 8, but the basic principle is that the statements in the super-sentence require a greater break between them than is provided by a comma but are too closely connected in sense to be separated completely by full stops.

A series of short sentences may be punctuated with commas:

I was thick, I was fat, I was useless at games, I wore old patched clothes, I smelt. No wonder I was unpopular at school.

These, too, can be considered super-sentences since there are no linking words connecting them, but the main type of super-sentence is the one punctuated with semicolons.

Reduced sentences

Reduced sentences are words or groups of words that do not have the full structure of simple sentences but are still independent units of speech:

What a lovely day!
Happy birthday!
Good morning.
Yes, please.

Reduced sentences are a normal feature of colloquial conversation:

'Are you serious?' **'Quite serious.'**
'He actually said that?' **'Those very words.'**
'What are you going to do about it?' **'Absolutely nothing.'**

Although not grammatically complete (they lack subjects and verbs), each of these highlighted sentences is
complete in itself in that it is perfectly clear from the
context what is meant:

'Are you serious?' **'I am quite serious.'**
'He actually said that?' **'He said those very words.'**
'What are you going to do about it?' **'I am going to do abso-
lutely nothing about it.'**

Here is another example of a conversation with reduced
sentences:

*Coffee? Tea? With milk? And sugar? How many lumps? How
about a biscuit? Or a cake, perhaps? One of those sticky,
chocolaty ones?*

In speech and colloquial writing, reduced sentences
like these are entirely natural. Reduced sentences are
less used in formal writing, but are acceptable in the
form of short comments:

Can the Coalition win the war? **Probably.** *Can they win the
peace?* **Possibly not.**
So much changes when children start school. **Everything, in
fact.**
*Only a brave or foolhardy MSP would propose a Scottish space-
exploration programme.* **But then again, why not?**

Non-sentences

> *She began many sentences without ending them,*
> *running them into one another, in much the same*
> *confused sort of way in which written words run*
> *together on blotting-paper.*
>
> Mrs Gaskell, *Cranford*

There are two categories of non-sentence, both the cause of and created by bad punctuation. They will be referred to as **fragments** and **strings**.

Fragments

• Structure

Fragments are groups of words that are really parts of sentences but which have been punctuated as if they were complete sentences.

Fragments differ from reduced sentences in that reduced sentences are independent of what precedes or follows them, while fragments, when you read them carefully, clearly belong together in a larger sentence that has simply been chopped up by inappropriate punctuation. Fragments can be recognized by their failure to meet the 'complete thought' test (see page 25) and by the clear grammatical links between them that show that they really belong together in a single sentence. Some examples will make this clearer. The following examples consist of fragments:

✗ *Knowing I would have to perform in front of an audience. I was extremely miserable.*

✗ *She stopped. Suddenly overcome by weariness. Owing to her great exertions in the intense heat.*

✗ *People who work in first-class restaurants and hotels have usually been trained in catering schools. Of which there are many.*

In the first example, the first fragment explains the reason for what is said in the second fragment. They therefore belong together in one sentence as a subordinate clause followed by a main clause:

✓ *Knowing I would have to perform in front of an audience, I was extremely miserable.*

Similarly, in the second example, the second fragment explains what is said in the first clause, and the third fragment expands on what is said in the second, so they should be linked together to form a single composite sentence consisting of a main clause followed by a subordinate clause:

✓ *She stopped, suddenly overcome by weariness owing to her great exertions in the intense heat.*

And in the third example, the fragment 'of which there are many' is clearly linked to 'catering schools', and the punctuation should reflect this:

✓ *People who work in first-class restaurants and hotels have usually been trained in catering schools, of which there are many.*

Fragments are acceptable as a representation of fragmented speech:

Don't you remember? When we first met? Long ago. That summer afternoon. In the park.
I wasn't worried. Not in the least. Not even for a moment.
Lovely marrows. Grew them myself. At the allotment.

And occasionally, a sentence may be split into fragments for the sake of emphasis. Compare the following two examples:

The crowd were cheering loudly, enthusiastically and passionately.
The crowd were cheering. Loudly. Enthusiastically. Passionately.

This is an acceptable literary device but it should not be overdone. Fragments are rarely acceptable in formal writing, and if you spot any in your own writing, give careful consideration to a possible rewrite.

Strings
• **Structure**

Strings are the opposite of fragments, and are far more common in poorly punctuated writing. In strings, two or more sentences are simply strung together, separated by commas where they should have stronger breaks indicated by full stops or at least semicolons (see **Super-sentences** above). Again, an example will make the point more clearly:

✗ *The occupier of a house in Park Crescent discovered his garage door open after he had previously secured it, nothing was reported stolen.*

There are two pieces of information here, two separate 'complete thoughts' if you like, with a change of topic (marked by ///):

The occupier of a house in Park Crescent discovered his garage door open after he had previously secured it /// nothing was reported stolen.

It is also clear that both what precedes the suggested break and what follows it form two grammatically complete sentences, each with a subject and verb. The correct punctuation for this passage is therefore as two separate sentences:

✓ *The occupier of a house in Park Crescent discovered his garage door open after he had previously secured it. Nothing was reported stolen.*

Sometimes the use of a comma where a full stop is needed leads to the omission of other commas that should have been inserted in the sentence. Compare the punctuation in the following examples:

✗ *Infant drinks may contain sugar which increases the risk of tooth decay, to reduce this and other related risks we recommend that you follow the advice below.*

✓ *Infant drinks may contain sugar, which increases the risk of tooth decay. To reduce this and other related risks, we recommend that you follow the advice below.*

✗ *I was walking along the road with my mobile phone in my hand talking to my daughter and this boy came along on a bike, snatched the phone from me and pushed me over. I must have seemed an easy target, it could happen to anyone. There was no-one else around, luckily there was a shop nearby where I went for help, a kind lady walked me home to make sure I was all right.*

✓ *I was walking along the road with my mobile phone in my*

hand, talking to my daughter, and this boy came along on a bike, snatched the phone from me and pushed me over. I must have seemed an easy target. It could happen to anyone. There was no-one else around. Luckily there was a shop nearby, where I went for help. A kind lady walked me home to make sure I was all right.

As a general rule, if you find that some of your sentences seem to be going on for rather a long time, always check to see whether you are actually writing strings.

Summary of key points

- There are four kinds of sentence: *simple sentences*, *composite sentences*, *super-sentences* and *reduced sentences*.
- Simple sentences have one subject and one main verb.
- Composite sentences consist of two or more simple sentences linked by at least one conjunction.
- Super-sentences are sentences composed of two or more simple or composite sentences that are too closely related in sense to be separated by a full stop.
- Reduced sentences are sentences that are grammatically incomplete but which are not linked to what precedes or follows.
- There are two kinds of non-sentence: *fragments* and *strings*.
- Fragments consist of elements that belong together in a single sentence but which have been punctuated as two or more sentences.
- Strings consist of two or more sentences that have been punctuated as a single sentence.

4
Full stops

*No iron can stab the heart with such force as a full
stop put just at the right place.*

Isaac Babel, *Guy de Maupassant*

A full stop is sometimes called a *period*. There are two
main uses of the full stop:

1. to mark the end of a sentence; and
2. to indicate an abbreviation.

Full stops in sentences

The basic rule

The basic rule for the use of the full stop is quite
straightforward:

*Use a full stop to mark the end of any complete sentence that
is neither a question nor an exclamation.*

What is or is not a 'complete sentence' has been explained in Chapter 3.

There are five punctuation marks that can be used
at the end of a sentence: the full stop (.), the question
mark (?), the exclamation mark (!), the dash (–) and

the ellipsis or omission mark (...). Of these five, the last four have specialized uses, indicating respectively questions, exclamations and, in the last two cases, incomplete sentences (see Chapters 5, 6, 10 and 13). The full stop is the punctuation mark to use at the end of a sentence unless there is a good reason for using any of the other four.

The coins were pure gold.
She smiled at the little girl.
We realized that we were not in immediate danger.
I have no intention of taking things easy when I retire.

Commands
Commands should end with full stops unless they express strong force or emotion, in which case they should be closed with an exclamation mark. Compare the following:

Come in. Take a seat.
Come in when I tell you! And sit down!

Statements, questions and requests
Some sentences that have the form of questions are in fact commands or requests and should be punctuated with a full stop rather than a question mark:

Could you close the door, please.
Would anyone who requires a return ticket please come to the purser's office on the main deck.

Similarly, there are sentences in the form of statements that are really questions. It is better to punctuate such sentences with a question mark rather than a full stop (though a full stop is usually considered correct too, and is actually preferred by some authorities – this is one of these grey areas in punctuation where personal taste applies more than rules):

James, I was wondering if you would like to come to the show with us?

But if a sentence is clearly a statement rather than a question, it should of course be punctuated with a full stop:

'What are you thinking about?' 'Oh, I was just wondering whether James would like to come to the show with us.'

At the end of a composite sentence that begins with a statement of fact but ends with a statement functioning as a question, you should use a full stop:

James, we have an extra ticket for the show and I was wondering if you would like to come with us.

On the other hand, if the sentence begins with a question and ends with something like 'I wonder', the whole sentence should be punctuated as a question:

Diamonds are carbon. Do they burn, I wonder?

Full stops replaced by commas in direct speech
When a speech verb follows a sentence of direct speech, the full stop at the end of the sentence is replaced by a comma:

'That remains to be seen,' said Gordon.
'I don't think that's very funny,' she said. 'It wasn't meant to be funny,' he muttered to himself.

However, in a sentence that follows the speech verb, the full stop remains:

'I don't think that's very funny,' she said. 'Don't ever do that again. I don't like it.'
'I love you,' he said. 'I love you, and I need you. I couldn't live without you. Not now. Not ever.'

Position of full stops beside parentheses and quotation marks

When words in parentheses form a complete and independent sentence, a full stop should go *inside* the closing parenthesis:

All the fish served in the restaurant is caught locally except for the prawns, which come from farther along the coast. (For some reason, they're a lot tastier than the local ones.)
He also drew the illustrations for this book. (That was something he very rarely did.)

When words in parentheses are a comment that form part of a sentence, the full stop should be outside the parentheses:

All the fish served in the restaurant is caught locally except for the prawns, which come from farther along the coast (and for some reason are a lot tastier than the local ones).
He also drew the illustrations for this book (which was something he very rarely did).

The same applies with quotation marks. Compare the following examples:

The sign said, 'Visitors Welcome'.
There was a sign at the front door. 'Visitors Welcome.'

A sign welcomed us to 'Prague, City of a Hundred Spires'.
The incident had been officially put down as an 'Act of God'.

American practice differs from British practice. In American English, the full stop always goes *inside* the closing quotation mark:

The incident had been officially put down as an "Act of God."

Omission of full stops

• **No full stop after direct speech ending in a punctuation mark**

When the end of a passage of direct speech coincides with the end of a sentence, there should logically be two punctuation marks, one inside the quotation marks to indicate the end of the direct speech and one outside the quotation marks to indicate the end of the whole sentence. However, in practice, when the second punctuation mark would have been a full stop, it is omitted:

✘ *I heard someone behind me in the queue say, 'My feet hurt.'.*
✓ *I heard someone behind me in the queue say, 'My feet hurt.'*
✘ *The lieutenant leapt to his feet, shouting: 'Charge!'.*
✓ *The lieutenant leapt to his feet, shouting: 'Charge!'*
✘ *I said to him, 'I beg your pardon? What did you say to me?'.*
✓ *I said to him, 'I beg your pardon? What did you say to me?'*

A dash marks a sentence that has come to an abrupt stop without being completed, and for that reason is not followed by a full stop:

My luggage has been –

In the case of an ellipsis mark (...) at the end of a sentence, it is correct to add a fourth dot as a full stop, but current practice favours the omission of the full stop, leaving just the three ellipsis points:

What on earth was he doing in there? We waited and waited ...

• **No full stop added after an abbreviation ending in a full stop**
If a sentence ends with an abbreviation that ends with a full stop (for example *Ph.D.*), the full stop marking the end of the sentence itself should be omitted (i.e. there should be only one full stop, not two):

✗ *I don't think I'll ever complete my Ph.D..*
✓ *I don't think I'll ever complete my Ph.D.*

• **No full stops in headlines, captions, titles, etc**
Newspaper headlines, picture captions, the titles of books, plays, songs and poems, sub-titles, chapter headings and section headings in reports, etc are not followed by a full stop, even if they are complete sentences:

Row over terror claim
Celebrities jump into the jungle
The secret message on this monument may finally be revealed this week
To a Skylark

However, should a headline, etc consist of two sentences, the first sentence should end with a full stop, although the second one will not:

He just walked out the door. That was the last time I saw him

Summary of key points

- Put a full stop at the end of any complete sentence that is not a question or an exclamation.
- Replace a full stop with a comma in direct speech before a speech verb.
- A sentence that has the form of a question but the function of a request or a command should end in a full stop.
- A sentence that has the form of a statement but the function of a question should usually end with a question mark.
- Headings, captions and titles should have no full stop even if they are full sentences.
- Do not add a full stop after another punctuation mark.

Full stops in abbreviations

There is a general tendency in British English to omit full stops in abbreviations nowadays, but it is not correct to omit them in every case. Where British English may equally correctly have or omit full stops in abbreviations, American English tends to use forms with full stops.

Abbreviations of words

Abbreviations that do not include the last letter of the abbreviated word are generally followed by a full stop:

adv., approx., cent. (= 'century'), *d.* (= 'died'), *doz., esp., Jan., masc., Sq., Tues., vol.,* etc

Frankly, I'm v. lukewarm about the whole business. (= 'very')

Nonetheless, many of these abbreviations (especially the days of the week and the months) are nowadays frequently written without full stops. This is now considered quite correct. (See page 52 for abbreviations of Latin words.)

Abbreviations that include the last letter of the shortened word are generally written without full stops in British English:

Mr, Mrs, Dr, St, Rd, etc

Full stops are not incorrect, though. (But write *Ms* without a full stop, because it is not actually an abbreviation: there is no word of which *Ms* is a shortened form.)

It is also sensible to add a full stop to any abbreviation that might be wrongly interpreted as a word. An example Carey gives in *Mind the Stop* is *coy.* for 'company' (in the armed forces), the full stop being needed to distinguish between a 'coy. commander' and a 'coy commander'.

Abbreviations formed with numbers are never followed by full stops:

1st, 2nd, 3rd, 4th, 4to (= 'quarto'), *8vo* (= 'octavo')

If an abbreviation of a singular word ends with a full stop, then its plural form generally also ends with a full stop:

ed. (= 'editor'), *eds.* (= 'editors'); *eds* is also correct

Abbreviations of names

Abbreviations of the names of countries, organizations, etc are usually written without full stops:

USA, UN, EU, etc

Full stops are not incorrect, though. But when the abbreviations are pronounced as words, they must not be written with full stops:

Nato, UNESCO, UNICEF, etc

Similarly *VAT*, when pronounced 'vat', must be written without full stops, but when it is pronounced 'vee ay tee' it can be written with or without full stops.

With people's initials it is equally correct to omit or write full stops, and in British English probably now commoner to omit them:

R B Burns or *R. B. Burns*

With abbreviations of names, whether or not including the final letter of the name, add a full stop:

Robt. Burns, Jas. Taylor, Geo. Davidson

Abbreviations of British county names are followed by full stops:

Hants., Leics., Yorks.

Some authorities prefer *Hants* and *Northants* without full stops, but there seems to be no good reason for making them exceptions to the general rule.

Abbreviations of states of the USA are also written with full stops, but not when part of a ZIP code:

S.D. or *S. Dak.* (= 'South Dakota') but *SD 15479*

There are no full stops in British postcodes:

WC2R ORL

Abbreviations of units of measurement

Abbreviations of units of metric measurement, of the temperature scales, and of compass directions, and the symbols for chemical elements are written without full stops:

cm, km, kg
10°C, 180°F
WSW, NNE
C, Fe, Pb, Z

Symbols such as £, *s, d, p* and $, ¢ are not followed by full stops, though it is correct to have full stops in £.*s.d.* (pronounced 'ell ess dee').

Abbreviations of units of non-metric measurement may be written with or without full stops:

in or *in.* (= 'inch'; the form with a full stop avoids possible confusion with the word 'in')

If the abbreviation includes the last letter of the word, there is usually no full stop:

ft, hr, mth, yr

Note also *lb* (= 'pound') and *oz* (= 'ounce').

If the abbreviation has a full stop in the singular, it will have one in the plural as well; if not in the singular, then not in the plural:

ins or *ins.* (but note that the abbreviation *in.* is also used for 'inches')

Other mathematical and scientific abbreviations are written with full stops:

d. (= diameter), etc

Authorities, however, sometimes disagree over whether a particular letter is an abbreviation (which may be written with a full stop) or a symbol (which is not followed by a full stop). If in doubt, follow the recommendations in your own dictionary or textbook.

Abbreviations of university degrees and public honours
Abbreviations of degrees and honours may be written with full stops, but are usually written without:

MA, BSc, PhD, MLitt, etc or *M.A., B.Sc., Ph.D., M.Litt.,* etc
OBE, KCVO, etc or *O.B.E.,* etc

Abbreviations of Latin words
Abbreviations of Latin words are usually written with full stops:

a.m., p.m., e.g., i.e., ibid., no., q.v., viz., etc

However, *etc* is now often written without a full stop (as it is in this book) and *eg* and *ie* sometimes are. The former is acceptable, the latter two better avoided. In stating times, both *a.m.* and *p.m.* and *am* and *pm* are acceptable: *at 12 p.m.* or *at 12 pm.* In all other cases, keep the full stops.

AD and BC (usually written as small capitals) may

be written with or without full stops, and nowadays more often without.

Other abbreviations

Other abbreviations written in capitals are nowadays generally written without full stops (though in most cases full stops are not wrong):

AGM, CD, CV, MOT, OK, PLC, VDU, etc

Two-letter abbreviations of single words

TV should not be written with full stops, because it is the abbreviation of the single word 'television'. However, *T.V.* has long been in common use, and for that reason possibly has to be considered acceptable, even if the full stops are unnecessary and illogical. The abbreviation *TV.*, with one full stop, though logically correct, has never caught on.

Similarly, *PS* or *ps* without full stops should be used for 'postscript', *MS* or *ms* for 'manuscript', *ID* for 'identity', and *TB* for 'tuberculosis'.

Texting, Internet and email abbreviations

Abbreviations used in texting, on the Internet and in email are not written with full stops:

BFN (= 'bye for now')
HAND (= 'have a nice day')

Summary of key points

- There are fewer full stops in abbreviations now than formerly.
- Except for personal names, abbreviations that include the last letter of a word need not be written with full stops.
- Abbreviations that are pronounced as words should not be written with full stops.
- Abbreviations of units of metric measurement, of the temperature scales, and of compass directions and the symbols for chemical elements are written without full stops.
- Abbreviations of Latin words are usually written with full stops.

Other uses of a full stop or dot

Decimal numbers and decimal currency

A full stop is often used instead of a centred dot in decimal numbers:

35.75%

A full stop is also written between the main unit and the smaller unit of a decimal currency:

£62.39, $104.26

Time

In British English, a full stop is written between the hours and the minutes in stating a time:

The train should arrive at 7.35.

In American English, a colon is regularly used in this position:

The train should arrive at 7:35.

With a 24-hour clock time, usage varies. There may be no punctuation at all (*1935*) – this is especially common in timetables; there may be a full stop (*19.35*); or there may be a colon (*19:35*).

When seconds are shown as well as hours and minutes, the general preference currently seems to be for colons (*19:35:05*).

Dots may also be written between the day, month and year of a date (*12.10.04*), though slashes are also possible (*12/10/04*).

Email and website addresses

Full stops or dots are used in email and website addresses (and of course are called 'dot' when the address is spelt out):

petenbabs@aol.com
www.labcoat.co.uk

5
Question marks

A kiss can be a comma, a question mark or an exclamation point.

Mistinguett (French comedienne)

Question marks in sentences

The basic rule
A question mark replaces a full stop at the end of any sentence that asks a direct question:

Have you got the receipt?
What time is it?
Can you remember what he actually said?

A question mark may be the only indication that a sentence is intended as a question. Compare

They're closing the supermarket. Next week.

and

They're closing the supermarket? Next week?

In a composite sentence, if only part of the sentence is a question and the rest a statement, the whole sentence requires a question mark:

When a lion escapes from a circus in Africa, how do they know when they've caught the right one?

George Carlin

What would you do if you thought you were being followed by a stalker?

Similarly, a question mark is used at the end of a sentence comprising a statement followed by a question tag:

I could hardly ask her that, could I?
You will be there, won't you?

Indirect questions

An indirect question does not actually ask a question; it says what the question is or was. It is therefore a statement, not a question, and should be punctuated with a full stop, not a question mark.

The following examples show three direct questions followed by the corresponding indirect questions:

'Do you need any help?' she asked.
'Where do you live, little girl?' she asked.
'What is she doing?' he wondered.
She asked whether he needed any help.
She asked the little girl where she lived.
He wondered what she was doing.

Questions, statements, requests and exclamations
Statements as questions

There are sentences in the form of indirect questions or other statements that *do* require to be followed by question marks, because they are in fact asking questions:

I wonder if you could tell me where the bus station is? (You are not actually wondering if the person knows where the bus station is, you are asking for directions to it.)

I suppose there's no hope of anyone having survived the explosion? (You are asking whether anyone might have survived the explosion.)

Surely Joanna must have known that her lavish lifestyle couldn't go on forever? (You are expressing surprise, anger, etc, by asking the reader or listener to agree with you that Joanna must have known this.)

I presume she got home all right? (You're asking for confirmation.)

A full stop is usually considered correct in this position too, and in fact some authorities prefer it. But the question mark seems logically better, since its job is to indicate a question and these sentences are questions.

This use of the question mark is acceptable with verbs of wondering or supposing, but it should not be used with verbs that do not actually ask questions:

✗ *I hope your mother is feeling a bit better?*
✓ *I hope your mother is feeling a bit better.*

At the end of a composite sentence that begins with a statement of fact but ends with a questioning statement, you should use a full stop:

I'm a bit short of cash this month and I was wondering if you could lend me £100.

A question mark is sometimes used to show that a sentence should be spoken with a rising, questioning intonation, as, for example, when the speaker is making a tentative suggestion:

Perhaps the letter has got lost in the post? (This is asking for agreement rather than just expressing an opinion.)

With a full stop indicating a falling intonation at the end of the sentence, the suggestion is less tentative and is not asking for agreement:

Perhaps the letter has got lost in the post.

Questions as requests

There are sentences in the *form* of questions that are not in fact questions at all. For example, they may be requests:

Could you pass me the salt, please. (You already know that the person could pass the salt, so this is a request, not a question. A request of this type is often said with a rising question-like intonation, so punctuation with a question mark is also correct.)
Would the owner of the Volkswagen Polo parked at the main gate please move it immediately.
May I take this opportunity of introducing myself.

A forceful request may even require an exclamation mark:

Will you knock off doing that!

Questions indicating surprise

A sentence in the form of a question may be used to express surprise, and in this case it should be punctuated with a full stop:

And who should we see at the hotel but Tom and Anne. What a surprise!

Questions and exclamations

Some sentences in the form of questions are actually exclamations, and should therefore be punctuated with exclamation marks:

Wasn't that a great concert! (This is not a question but a strong expression of an opinion.)

The same sentence may therefore be punctuated differently depending on its underlying meaning:

What are you doing? (question requesting information)
What are you doing! (exclamation expressing anger, surprise, horror, etc)

A rule of thumb

When in doubt, punctuate a sentence according to its *meaning* or *intention* rather than its grammatical form.

Question marks in a series of repeated part questions

In a series of full and reduced question sentences, each sentence requires a question mark (and must also begin with a capital letter):

If the house was occupied, would the owner phone the police? Attack us with an axe? Shoot us?

An alternative would be to treat these sentences as parts of a single sentence and punctuate accordingly:

If the house was occupied, would the owner phone the police, attack us with an axe, or shoot us?

Punctuation as three separate sentences suggests that these are just three random possibilities being considered; there could be others. Punctuation as a single sentence suggests that there are *only* these three possibilities, or at least that these are the only three being considered at that moment.

Some writers break what are technically single question sentences into two or more parts:

Were these heresies the consequences of attempts to add alien elements onto a Christian foundation? Or the result of fitting elements of Christianity into a prior non-Christian religious system?

Notice that in this example the second 'sentence' beginning with 'Or' has no subject or verb. It is in fact a fragment (see page 36). If the writer wanted to make a break between the two questions, he could have repeated the subject and verb:

*Were these heresies the consequences of attempts to add alien elements onto a Christian foundation? Or **were they** the result of fitting elements of Christianity into a prior non-Christian religious system?*

Alternatively, the two questions could have been merged into one:

*Were these heresies the consequences of attempts to add alien elements onto a Christian foundation, **or** the result of fitting elements of Christianity into a prior non-Christian religious system?*

You may even see part sentences in a series without initial capital letters:

[✗] *So then, where does that leave the wise? or the scholars? or the skilful debaters of this world?*

Good News Bible, 1 Corinthians 1:20

Again, this seems an unnecessary and undesirable half-way house. Either the fragments should be formed into a single sentence or else, if greater emphasis is required, they should be treated as fully separate sentences and punctuated accordingly:

[✓] *So then, where does that leave the wise, or the scholars, or the skilful debaters of this world?*

[✓] *So then, where does that leave the wise? Or the scholars? Or the skilful debaters of this world?*

Questions embedded in statements

Note the punctuation of the following examples:

What will happen now? is the question on everyone's lips.
The question on everyone's lips is, what will happen now?

Opinion is divided on the acceptability of sentences such as these without further, or different, punctuation. The first example would certainly be improved by the addition of quotation marks:

'What will happen now?' is the question on everyone's lips.

The second example is generally considered acceptable as it is, but it could equally well be written with quotation marks, in which case the question must start with a capital letter:

The question on everyone's lips is, 'What will happen now?'

There is no full stop after the closing quotation mark:
see **Omission of punctuation marks** below. The
comma after 'is' is optional, but it is probably better
to put one in as indicative of the short pause that will
usually be left between 'is' and 'what' when the sentence is spoken.

With a verb of wondering or supposing, the whole
sentence can be considered the question (compare
Statements as questions page 57), so the question mark
should be at the end of the sentence:

Where is she, I wonder?
He's down the pub again, I suppose?

If the embedded question is not in the actual form the
question would have when spoken (compare **Indirect
questions** page 57), then the sentence should be punctuated as a statement with a comma and a full stop:

What would happen next, was the question on everyone's lips.
The question on everyone's lips was, what would happen next.
Where was she, I wondered.

Headlines, captions, titles, etc
Unlike full stops (see page 47), question marks are not
omitted from newspaper headlines, picture captions,
the titles of books, plays, songs and poems, sub-titles,
chapter headings and section headings in reports, etc:

Does passive smoking kill?
Have You Seen My Pretty Peggy?

Position of question marks with quotation marks and parentheses

In questions in direct speech enclosed in quotation marks, the question mark stands *inside* the quotation marks:

'What does your dog look like?' she asked.

Unlike the full stop (see page 44), the question mark is not replaced by a comma in this position:

✗ *'What does your dog look like,' she asked.*

Nor is it followed by a comma:

✗ *'What does your dog look like?,' she asked.*
✗ *'What does your dog look like?', she asked.*

When a question mark comes at the end of a sentence immediately after a word or words that are highlighted by quotation marks, the question mark should follow the closing quotation mark:

Is it the duty of an artist to 'keep out of politics'?

American English does not differ from British English here (compare the rules for full stops and commas on pages 46 and 126):

Is it the duty of an artist to "keep out of politics?"

In the case of parentheses, simple logic applies. If the question mark belongs to the sentence as a whole, it should go outside the parentheses:

Was it not in this very bar that he had ordered 'Twenty Bloody Marys' (but not all for himself, of course)?

If the question mark belongs to a question within parentheses, the question mark goes inside the parentheses too:

He loved her as a woman (who could not?) but also as his muse.

The same applies to a question inserted as a comment between dashes:

She was obviously slightly – how shall I put it? – 'tired and emotional'.

Omission of punctuation marks

When the end of a passage of direct speech coincides with the end of a sentence, there should logically be two punctuation marks, one inside the quotation marks to indicate the end of the direct speech and one outside the quotation marks to indicate the end of the sentence. However, in practice, when the second punctuation mark would have been a full stop, it is omitted:

I said to him, 'What on earth was that noise?'

If one of the punctuation marks is a question mark and the other is an exclamation mark, neither is dropped:

Why did you shout, 'Look out for that car!'?
Stop saying, 'Why? Why? Why?'!

If the two punctuation marks are both question marks, they may both be kept, but alternatively one or other of them can be dropped:

Why did she say, 'Who are you?'?
Why did she say, 'Who are you?'

Why did she say, 'Who are you'?

Clearly, if a question mark is the only indication that a sentence is a question, it cannot be dropped. Compare these examples:

Who was the girl who screamed, 'George Bush has won again?'
Who was the girl who screamed, 'George Bush has won again!'?

Multiple punctuation marks

Sometimes a question mark may be repeated or followed by one or more exclamation marks:

Did he really say that?? Really?!!

This is acceptable in informal writing as a representation of a speaker's emotion and intonation, but it should *never* be used in formal writing. In general, there should only one punctuation mark at the end of the sentence.

Summary of key points

- End a direct question with a question mark, but an indirect question with a full stop.
- When there is a clash between the form of a sentence and its meaning or intention, punctuate it according to its meaning or intention.
- With regard to quotation marks and parentheses, place the question marks at the end of the question they belong to.

Other uses of question marks

Uncertainty

A question mark in parentheses may be used to draw attention to something that the writer is uncertain about or which seems suspicious or questionable:

The arbitrary(?) doubling of letters is a feature of these inscriptions. (The use of (?) here indicates that the writer is not sure whether the doubling of letters in the inscriptions is in fact arbitrary. It may be, but it may not be.)

Similarly, a question mark is used to indicate that a given date is not certain. There is more than one correct style for this:

The Pharaoh fled to Ethiopia in 340(?) BC.
The Pharaoh fled to Ethiopia in (?)340 BC.

Geoffrey Chaucer (?1340–1400) wrote The Canterbury Tales. Among the British authors he quotes are Sir Thomas Elyot (?1490–1546) and Thomas Cooper (?1517–1594).

If you want to suggest a correction to someone else's text, this should be done in *square* brackets:

The Pharaoh fled to Ethiopia in 340 [339?] BC.
The Pharaoh fled to Ethiopia in 340 [?339] BC.
(The original writer said 340 BC but the person quoting him thinks it was probably in 339 BC.)

6
Exclamation marks

The exclamation mark is the literary equivalent of a man holding up a card reading LAUGHTER to a studio audience.

Miles Kington

Exclamation marks in sentences

The basic use

An exclamation mark (also called an 'exclamation point' in American English) is used in place of a full stop to express emphasis or strong emotion:

What a mess!
Ouch! That hurts!
You swine!
I didn't do it! It wasn't me!
'No!' she screamed. 'I don't want your money!'

An exclamation mark is often used to emphasize the depth of feeling in a sentence, especially in informal writing such as personal letters and emails:

It was lovely to be with you last weekend!
Great news! That's excellent! Well done!

This has been criticized by both G V Carey and Loreto Todd in their books as 'gushing', but it seems a harmless enough practice in informal personal letters and emails. If you want to do it, then go ahead and do it (but don't overdo it: Fowler says in *Modern English Usage* that 'excessive use of exclamation marks is ... one of the things that betray the uneducated or unpractised writer').

Precisely because it expresses strong emotion, the exclamation mark is not much used in formal writing, such as essays and reports, which requires a more measured and objective style of writing.

Commands

A command should only be followed by an exclamation mark when it expresses strong emotion:

Don't speak to me like that!
Don't touch me!

Otherwise a command is correctly followed by a full stop:

Please sit down.
Don't change anything. Leave the room as it is.

Exclamation marks in poetry

In poetry, the name of a person being addressed is often followed by an exclamation mark:

Dear child! Dear girl! that walkest with me here . . .

William Wordsworth, 'By the Sea'

Milton! thou shouldst be living at this hour . . .

William Wordsworth, 'London, 1802'

O World! O Life! O Time!
On whose last steps I climb . . .

Percy Bysshe Shelley, 'A Lament'

Notice that what follows the exclamation mark begins with a lower-case letter, not a capital, except (as in the third example) when the word begins a new line, which in poetry normally requires a capital letter.

Mid-sentence exclamations

Exclamations may come in the middle of sentences and should be punctuated with exclamation marks, but what follows the exclamation need not have a capital letter:

Nothing had been stolen, but oh, dear! what a mess there was.

You cannot hope
to bribe or twist,
thank God! the
British journalist.
But, seeing what
the man will do
unbribed, there's
no occasion to.

Humbert Wolfe, *The Uncelestial City*

Position of exclamation marks with quotation marks and parentheses

In exclamations in direct speech enclosed in quotation marks, the exclamation mark stands *inside* the quotation marks:

'That's not fair!' she shouted.

Unlike the full stop (see page 44), the exclamation mark is not replaced by a comma in this position:

✗ *'That's not fair,' she shouted.*

Nor is it followed by a comma:

✗ *'That's not fair!,' she shouted.*
✗ *'That's not fair!', she shouted.*

When an exclamation mark comes at the end of a sentence immediately after a word or words highlighted by quotation marks, it should follow the closing quotation mark:

How dare you call her a 'gorilla'!

American English does not differ from British English here (compare the rules for full stops and commas on pages 46 and 126):

How dare you call her a "gorilla"!

With parentheses, do what is logical. If the exclamation mark belongs to the sentence as a whole, it should go outside the parentheses, but if it belongs to an exclamation within parentheses, it goes inside the parentheses too:

Was it not in this very bar that he had ordered 'Twenty Bloody Marys' (but not all for himself, of course!).
He said he loved me not just as a woman but (oh, Lord!) also as his muse.

The same applies to a question inserted as a comment between dashes:

She was slightly drunk and – how typical! – very patronizing.

Multiple punctuation marks

In informal writing, especially in quotations of direct speech, an exclamation mark may be repeated to indicate a speaker's strong emotion or loudness:

Look out!!!

There may also be a mixture of punctuation marks:

He did what?!!

This is acceptable only in *informal* writing, and should in any case not be overdone. Formal writing, being more objective, rarely requires or allows the expression of emotion by means of even a single exclamation mark.

Questions, exclamations and requests

When there is a clash between the form of a sentence and its meaning, it is the meaning that governs the choice of punctuation mark:

Wasn't that awful! (This is an exclamation, not a question.)
What are you doing! (This is an exclamation of surprise, not a question.)

Will you stop doing that! (This is a forceful request.)

Of course, a genuine question must be punctuated with a question mark:

What are you doing?
Will he ever stop doing that?

With requests ending in question tags, an exclamation mark indicates a more forceful request than a question mark:

Have a word with him, will you?
Stop doing that, will you!

Omission of full stops
When the end of a passage of direct speech coincides with the end of a sentence, there should logically be two punctuation marks, one inside the quotation marks to indicate the end of the direct speech and one outside the quotation marks to indicate the end of the sentence. However, in practice, when the second punctuation mark would have been a full stop, it is omitted:

The lieutenant leapt to his feet, shouting: 'Charge!'
From the outside, the building doesn't look very inviting. You get a feeling of 'Keep out!'

When there is a question mark and a exclamation mark, both should be retained:

Why didn't you shout, 'Fore!'?

Headlines, captions, titles, etc

Unlike full stops (see page 47), exclamation marks are not omitted from newspaper headlines, picture captions, the titles of books, plays, songs and poems, sub-titles, chapter headings and section headings in reports, etc:

It's Party Time!
Look Who's Coming for Christmas!

Exclamation marks in emails

A recent development in punctuation is the use of the exclamation mark in salutations in emails where a comma would be expected in a letter:

Hi Norah!
Thanks for your email. . . .

This seems unexceptionable in informal emails, but do not do it in more formal settings:

Dear Mrs Brown,
Thank you for your email. . . .

(For further information on punctuating letters and emails, see page 261.)

Other uses of the exclamation mark

Indicating humour

> *Cut out all these exclamation points. An exclamation point is like laughing at your own joke.*

F Scott Fitzgerald

Scott Fitzgerald is perhaps too critical here. An exclamation mark may usefully and correctly be used to indicate that something is not intended to be taken seriously:

There have been some very odd things happening round here. We'll be seeing spaceships and little green men next!
I'd like to thank Norma for her unfailing good humour, even when I got things wrong!

The exclamation mark indicates to your reader that what you have said *is* a joke – you are not laughing at your own joke, you are inviting the reader to laugh at it. In speaking, this would be conveyed by facial expressions, gestures and intonation, but in writing the exclamation mark has to be brought in to do the job.

Indicating surprise

An exclamation mark in parentheses is used to show the writer's surprise at what is being said. The exclamation mark should follow the word or phrase that the reader's attention is being drawn to:

She said she was in the most enjoyable (!) of black depressions.

If the surprise is that of someone else who is quoting this sentence, then the exclamation mark should be in square brackets (see page 188 for further explanation of this point):

She said she was in the most enjoyable [!] of black depressions.

Indicating scorn

An exclamation mark may be used to indicate a sneering or scornful tone:

He even eats peas with his fingers!

Emphasis

An exclamation mark may be used to emphasize a comment:

On the (very rare!) occasions when she misunderstood something, she was always happy to be corrected.

Summary of key points

- An exclamation mark is used to indicate strong force or emotion.
- A command should be punctuated with a full stop, unless it is a forceful command, in which case an exclamation mark is correct.
- A sentence that has the form of a question but the force of an exclamation should be punctuated with an exclamation mark.
- Exclamation marks can be used to indicate humour, surprise or scorn, and can also be used for emphasis.

7
Commas

*Camilla, you see, wrote as she spoke; and her
indifference to the comma was legendary.*

Richard Mason, *The Drowning People*

The comma is probably the most important of all the
punctuation marks. It is certainly the most misused.
People who are weak at punctuation may scatter commas across the page in the hope that by so doing they
will have adequately punctuated their text, but it won't
work. To punctuate correctly, you cannot be indifferent to the comma. Indeed, if Camilla *really* wrote as
she spoke, she could not have been indifferent to her
commas at all, because commas often provide crucial
clues in a written text as to how something was said
or should be said, and therefore to its meaning.

It has been said that you cannot learn the use of the
comma by rule, and that is certainly true. More than
any other punctuation mark, the comma requires you
to use your own skill and judgement, and an understanding of broad principles as much as hard-and-fast
rules. But there *are* rules that can be learnt, and the
broad principles are very much a matter of common
sense.

This is a long chapter, so let's start off by stating four basic principles regarding commas:

1. The function of the comma is to make a slight break in a sentence, for any of a variety of reasons.
2. A comma often stands where there would be a slight pause in the spoken sentence.
3. It is correct, and necessary, to insert a comma anywhere it is needed to clarify the structure or meaning of a sentence.
4. The presence or absence of a comma may be the only way of conveying the correct meaning of a sentence.

When *not* to insert a comma

Many sentences do not require any breaks or pauses at all, and therefore do not need commas. Look, for example, at these simple sentences (for what a 'simple sentence' is, see page 26):

A flicker of doubt passed across his face.
There was a young man loitering at the corner.
I wandered across the grass to the castle.
We went off to have a cup of coffee and a sticky bun.

. . . and these composite sentences composed of main clauses (see page 31):

Sheila washed the dishes and Tom dried them.
I put my clothes in the locker and shut the door.
We laughed and sang the whole day long.
Either come inside or go away.
Jack had just had a heart attack but he still came to the meeting.

... and these composite sentences composed of a main clause followed by a subordinate clause (see page 30):

I'll forgive him because I love him.
We've got to get out of here before anyone sees us.
The children all hid under the bed when their mother came upstairs.
This is worse than I thought.
I told you he wouldn't come.
Here's another fine mess you've got me into.

Even quite long composite sentences may not need commas so long as they are clear and do not fall into any of the categories discussed below:

I'd been living in America for several years when I decided to pack in my job and head back home to Scotland to make this film.
We'd been in the sea for hours and were very cold and could hardly stand.

Comma separating subject and verb
It was formerly correct to insert a comma after the subject of the sentence if the subject was a clause or included a clause:

A man who has not been in Italy, is always conscious of an inferiority.

Samuel Johnson

One should never trust a woman who tells one her real age. A woman who would tell one that, would tell one anything.

Oscar Wilde

Nowadays, a parlour maid as ignorant as Queen Victoria was when she came to the throne, would be classed as mentally defective.

George Bernard Shaw

However, nowadays this use of the comma is generally felt to be incorrect:

✗ *That he should have achieved such a remarkable feat in two weeks, is simply incredible.*
✓ *That he should have achieved such a remarkable feat in two weeks is simply incredible.*

For some exceptions to this rule, see **Pauses** (page 97).

When to insert a comma

The following pages may seem daunting, filled as they are with structures and rules and exceptions. However, there are *three basic principles* that underpin everything that follows, easily learned and straightforward to apply:

1. Commas are used to split up sentences into smaller parts. To do this, commas should be added at sensible, logical breaks in sentences (for example, between clauses or round words that have been inserted into a clause). If you look carefully at the *structure* of your sentences, it will usually be clear where you should put the commas.
2. Commas often indicate where there are *pauses* in sentences. If in doubt about a comma, apply the 'pause test'. Say the sentence to yourself, and if you hear a pause, put in a comma (and if you don't

hear a pause, there is probably no need for a comma).
3. A comma could often be replaced by the word 'and'. This is the '*and* test'.

There are many more sentence structures in English than could possibly be discussed even in a chapter as long as this one is. But everything that follows in this chapter is based on these three principles, and if you apply them you should be able to deal with any problem you meet.

Subordinate clause + main clause

When a subordinate clause follows a main clause, there is usually no need for a comma. But a subordinate clause *preceding* the main clause is often separated from it by a comma:

When he awoke, there was a dog watching him.
If anything can go wrong, it will.
As she fell, she cried out in pain.
Because I love him, I'll forgive him.

It is usually better to put in the comma. However, when (a) there is a close connection in sense or topic between the clauses, (b) the subject of the verb in each clause is the same, and (c) there would be no pause between the clauses when spoken, then it is perfectly acceptable to omit the comma:

As she fell she cried out in pain.
As he sat up he could smell something burning.
Before I set off on my travels I spent one last evening with Frances.

Once inside the hutch the fox created havoc among the hens.
(= 'Once it was inside the hutch, the fox created . . .')

If these conditions are not met, there must be a comma; for example, with a change of subject:

When he got back, his wife was waiting for him.
Because I love him, he can get away with almost anything.

The longer the initial clause, the better it is to have a comma after it:

As we rushed up to the platform, we saw the train pulling out of the station.
If you have any pretensions to intellectual credibility, you don't ever want to be caught reading books of that sort.

When the subordinate clause includes a participle (a word ending in *-ing, -ed, -en*, etc) or an infinitive (a verb following 'to'), it should be followed by a comma:

Feeling rather peckish, she tiptoed downstairs to the kitchen.
Breathing heavily, he made his way across the garden.
Her hands raised to protect her face, she tried to back away.
Absolutely shaken by the experience, she lay down on the settee.

. . . though some authorities accept *-ing* clauses and infinitives without a comma:

While walking home after the party she was knocked down by a car.
To stop himself laughing he bit his lip hard.

Without any verb, there should be a comma:

Rather peckish, she tiptoed downstairs to the kitchen.
Quite out of breath, she collapsed at the side of the road.

Lastly, notice the difference in meaning the punctuation indicates in the following examples:

Pat having lost her keys, Gavin had to climb in through the bathroom window.
Pat, having lost her keys, had to climb in through the bathroom window.

To sum up this section: when in doubt, put a comma between a subordinate clause and a following main clause. It is not wrong to do so and sometimes wrong not to.

Main clause + subordinate clause

When a subordinate clause's only verb is a participle (a word ending in *-ing*, *-ed*, *-en*, etc), it should be separated from a preceding main clause by a comma:

She stepped towards him, looking mockingly into his eyes.
We tried various techniques, some turning out to be quite useful and some not.

A comma is often inserted before a subordinate clause to mark a pause (and a difference in meaning). Compare

I'm not going because I want to. Oh, no. I'm only going because I have to.

and

I'm not going, because I don't want to.

Main clause + linking word + main clause

When two main clauses are linked by a conjunction (*and, but, or,* etc), there is often no need for a comma between them. For example, there is no comma when one subject is linked to two or more verbs:

We laughed and laughed.
The crowd clapped and cheered and whistled.

. . . though commas may be used to indicate slight pauses for emphasis (see page 99):

She wept, and pleaded, and kissed his feet, and tore her clothes, but all to no avail.

Commas are also unnecessary when the themes of the linked clauses are closely connected:

Sheila washed the dishes and Tom dried them. (= one single activity – doing the dishes)
Winter came and the river froze over. (a single theme: the river froze *because* it was winter)
I shouted and shouted and shouted but nobody heard me. (describing a single situation, so no commas; but there could equally well be a comma before 'but' because of the contrast between 'I shouted' and 'nobody heard me' – see page 85)

A comma is generally used when the subject of the verb is different in each clause and/or the themes of each clause are not closely linked. Again there is likely to be a slight pause between the clauses:

Night fell, and it began to rain. (It didn't begin to rain because night had fallen; these are just two facts.)
I had a splitting headache, but we had to get the wallpapering

finished. (The headache and the wallpapering are not related.)
The fox sniffed the air for a moment, then trotted off across the field.

A comma may be needed between main clauses if they are long clauses. What exactly constitutes a 'long clause' is a matter of personal judgement. Here is an example without a comma, where it might have been better to have had one after 'night':

☒ *My need for somewhere to carry on with my writing without being disturbed was clearly of less importance than her need to entertain friends at all hours of the day and night and our relationship soon deteriorated to one of constant argument, accusation and recrimination.*
✓ *My need for somewhere to carry on with my writing without being disturbed was clearly of less importance than her need to entertain friends at all hours of the day and night, and our relationship soon deteriorated to one of constant argument, accusation and recrimination.*

A comma is often inserted between clauses to emphasize a contrast, particularly with *but* or *yet*:

I like maths, but my brother prefers English.
He seemed happy, yet there was obviously something bothering him.

. . . or to express a consequence, for example with *so*:

She goes out to work, so her mother looks after the children after school.
I was late in leaving the office, so was very lucky to find a taxi.

. . . but not with *and*:

Do that again and I'll smack you.

Don't agonize over all this. Just remember the general principles (same or different subjects, connected or unconnected themes, contrast or no contrast) and you won't go far wrong. And remember also to use the 'pause test' (page 80) if you are uncertain whether or not to insert a comma.

• **Comma or semicolon?**
Only a few linking words (*and, but, for, or, nor, so, while* and *yet*) can be preceded by a clause-separating comma:

My aunt is visiting us next week, and my cousins are joining us the following weekend.
I've not been well, but I'm better now.
Stop that now, or there'll be trouble.
She works the night shift, so she's always asleep in the morning.
John is a country boy at heart, while Sarah is definitely a townie.
He was a clever lad, yet he still failed all his exams.

Other connecting words (such as *also, consequently, for example, furthermore, hence, however, instead, moreover, nevertheless, therefore* and *thus*) must be preceded by a semicolon, and are usually followed by a comma:

Mandarin Ducks form a strong attachment to their partners and are said to pine away when they die; hence, they are also an emblem of conjugal fidelity.
He knew they would be looking for him; consequently, he had a preference for being in large crowds.

Churchill was a great man; moreover, he had a sense of history.
She had worked for the company for over twenty years; nevertheless, she got nothing from them when they made her redundant last month.
Owen renamed the town New Harmony; however, it was anything but harmonious.

These sentences could be punctuated with full stops rather than semicolons, but the semicolons are used to show the close connection between the two parts of each sentence. (For more on this, see page 131.)

If there is both a linking word such as *and* or *but* and a word such as *consequently, moreover*, etc, a comma is used:

He knew they would be looking for him, and consequently he had a preference for being in crowds.
Churchill was a great man, and moreover he had a sense of history.

When *consequently, moreover, nevertheless*, etc are inserted *into* clauses rather than standing as links between clauses, they are punctuated with two commas:

This book didn't move as fast as the others, but it was, nevertheless, a good read.
She was a great pianist. She was, moreover, a dedicated teacher.

Nevertheless and *consequently* can stand without commas if the contrast is expressed without stress or pauses:

This book didn't move as fast as the others, but it was nevertheless a good read.

She read a lot, and was consequently very knowledgeable about current affairs.

At the beginning of a sentence, there may or may not be a comma after words in this group; it depends on whether there is a pause (use the 'pause test'; see page 80).

That piece of land has been fought over for centuries. Consequently no-one plants anything there.
That piece of land has been fought over for centuries. Consequently, no-one plants anything there.
The theory is simple yet powerful. Nevertheless, it has its limitations.
I don't want to do it. Nevertheless I will.

Other sentence-initial words that make links between sentences are generally followed by commas:

We were too tired to go skinny-dipping with the others. Besides, who would want to?
It was apparently a pretty awful game. All the same, I wish I'd been there.
Firstly, the idea is impractical. Secondly, we don't have the money.

• **More about** *however*
Punctuation mistakes with *however* are particularly common, with commas instead of semicolons. These examples of incorrect punctuation are typical:

✗ *Her family were invited to her wedding, however the invitations were not even acknowledged.*

✗ *She knew there was no-one around, however she still kept looking over her shoulder to check.*

Here are the same examples correctly punctuated:

✓ *Her family were invited to her wedding; however, the invitations were not even acknowledged.*
✓ *She knew there was no-one around; however, she still kept looking over her shoulder to check.*

At the beginning of a sentence, *however* is always followed by a comma:

I'm really rather annoyed with her. However, I won't say anything.

When *however* is inserted *into* a clause rather than acting as a link between clauses, it is correctly punctuated with commas:

Things were, however, not quite going to plan.
We thought we heard someone walking about on the roof. It was, however, only a crow.

Note the difference in punctuation between *however* meaning 'nevertheless' and *however* meaning 'no matter how much':

I'm really annoyed with her. However, much as I want to, I won't say anything.
However much I want to, I won't say anything.

The relationship between the brain and the body, however, interesting in itself, is not our concern here. (= 'although interesting, the study of the relationship is nevertheless not our concern')

The relationship between the brain and the body, however interesting in itself, is not our concern here. (= 'the study is not our concern, no matter how interesting it is')

Main clauses not linked by conjunctions

When three or more main clauses are juxtaposed without conjunctions, they are separated by commas:

Nothing ever happens round here, no-one visits us, no-one writes, no-one phones.
You can do it, you must do it, you shall do it.
I like maths, my brother likes history, my sister prefers languages.
I'm going up to Findhorn, I'm going to talk to the plants and trees, I'm going to find inner peace and spiritual enlightenment – that's what I'm going to do.

It is generally considered wrong, however, to separate only two clauses by a comma. Unless there is a conjunction linking them, two clauses should be separated by a semicolon:

✗ *I like maths, my brother likes English.*
✓ *I like maths; my brother likes English.*
✓ *I like maths, and my brother likes English.*

You can, however, use a comma between two closely related and balanced parts of a sentence when the first one has a negative word (such as *not*) in it and the second one is a comment on the first:

I don't hate your cats, it's just that I'm a dog person.
These ideas weren't just misguided, they were criminally insane.

Even when the main clauses have subordinate clauses attached to them, commas are acceptable (though semicolons would not be wrong):

I can't confirm that there was a plot, I can only say that I was told that there was.
It's not that I'm afraid to die, I just don't want to be there when it happens.

Woody Allen, *Without Feathers*

Clauses expressing contrasts definitely require semicolons unless there is a linking word between them:

There are some people who are strongly opposed to women bishops; personally, I have no trouble with the idea.
There are some people who are strongly opposed to women bishops, but personally I have no trouble with the idea.

Fronting

If a word or phrase is brought forward to the beginning of a sentence for emphasis, it is usually not followed by a comma:

Sport they call it! I call it murder. (= 'they call it sport')
Really good soup it was too. (= 'it was really good soup')
Her poetry I like, but her short stories do nothing for me.
Einstein he ain't, but he's a good lad.

A clause in this position is often followed by a comma:

What he thought he was doing, heaven only knows. (= 'Heaven only knows what he thought he was doing')

Phrases saying when, where and how

> The American writer James Thurber was once asked
> why there was a comma in the sentence "After dinner,
> the men went into the living room." He replied that
> the comma had been inserted by Harold Ross, the
> editor of the New Yorker, and that the comma was
> Ross's way of giving the men time to push back their
> chairs and stand up.

A Thurber story quoted by many writers on punctuation

Thurber and Ross were forever arguing over commas,
but in this case both men were right. After an initial
word or phrase stating the time of action, it is equally
correct to insert a comma or to omit one. Here are
some examples without a comma:

By that time they had all left.
Every day the news got worse.
In the morning I awoke to find it was raining.
Presently they were joined by a third figure in black.
About eight o'clock we were picked up by some fishermen.

. . . and here are some with commas:

By that time, I was totally hooked on research.
In the morning, I got up early to have a look around the town.
Presently, she is a teacher in a city-centre school.
At about eight o'clock, we went back to Mum's for tea.

There may of course be more than one time phrase,
in which case it is better to put in the commas:

*Early the next morning, about eight o'clock, we left the camp
and went into the nearby town.*

The longer the initial phrase or phrases, the better it is to break up the sentence with a comma or two, but there is no hard-and-fast rule about this: it is a matter of your own taste and judgement. But here again, remember the 'pause test' (page 80).

When the time phrase comes at the end of the clause or sentence, there is no comma:

We left the hotel at about seven o'clock in the morning and drove south.

Words and phrases stating 'where' at the beginning of a sentence are, like those stating 'when', equally well written with or without a following comma:

Outside in the street a crowd was gathering.
Further along the road, there was a chip-shop.

Words and phrases describing 'how' are generally separated off by a comma at the beginning of a sentence but not at the end:

In panic, they took to their heels.
They took to their heels in panic.

Interruptions and add-ons
Any word or group of words that interrupts the structure of a clause must be separated off by commas:

Any alteration to the plans, however small, must be viewed as a victory.
He has, among other things, a black belt in karate.
Why is it, incidentally, that swimming pools are always such unattractive buildings?
It is, of course, not quite as simple as that.

She is, after all, his mother.
That, you see, is the problem we're up against.
I was, as you may gather, slightly annoyed with her.
I'm very fond of, but allergic to, long-haired cats.
This war, like the next war, is a war to end war.

Lloyd George

An Englishman, even if he is alone, forms an orderly queue of one.

George Mikes

Always make sure both commas are there. Watch especially in long sentences where you may simply forget the second one:

✗ *Repeated invasion of their country by foreign armies over the centuries, and the accompanying outrages and atrocities that had been inflicted upon them had given rise to a particularly strong stoicism among the peasants.*
✓ *Repeated invasion of their country by foreign armies over the centuries, and the accompanying outrages and atrocities that had been inflicted upon them had given rise to a particularly strong stoicism among the peasants.*

Similarly, a word or group of words added on at the beginning or end of a sentence needs to be separated off by a comma:

Of course, it is not quite as simple as that.
Between you and me, I'm not very impressed.
Frankly, I couldn't care less.
Like sheep, they all do the same thing.
Really, what is to become of you?
Excuse me, is this the Birmingham train?

Well, Bob, what do you think?
Well now, what have you been up to?
Hey, I hear you've got a new car.
That's the problem, you see.
I saw Kate yesterday, by the way.
I'm not quite sure what happened, to tell you the truth.
It could only happen in Ireland, and it did. In Donegal, to be precise.
He stared at her, totally unnerved by her bizarre behaviour.
She stared at him, her face as white as a sheet.
There were a lot of escape attempts, some successful, some not.
It's broken, I'm afraid.
So you've got a new car, eh?
Are you coming with us, Sam?
Good morning, sir.
Sleep all right, did you?
That's great news, isn't it?
Yes, please.
No, thank you.

Moving a subject and verb from the start of a sentence to the middle or end of the sentence turns them into insertions or add-ons:

I thought it was a ridiculous waste of time.
It was, I thought, a ridiculous waste of time.
I suppose you could argue that they were just showing some initiative.
You could argue, I suppose, that they were just showing some initiative.
I think he got the message.
He got the message, I think.

As a general rule, any element of a sentence that is not strictly connected to what precedes or follows requires a comma to mark the separation. Sometimes the sense of the sentence changes according to whether or not part of it is treated as an add-on:

The girls wanted to stay till Julian arrived. (because they liked Julian)
The girls wanted to stay, till Julian arrived. (because they didn't like Julian)

You should have planted the bush as I told you. (= 'I told you how to plant it')
You should have planted the bush, as I told you. (= 'I told you to plant it')

Commas, brackets and dashes

Commas are not the only way of separating off comments in a sentence. Both dashes and brackets are used for this purpose too:

The bus stopped frequently – every 20 feet in places, it seemed – and at nearly every stop there was a large exchange of people.
Its seafront promenade is handsome and well maintained and its vast bay (174 square miles, if you're taking notes) is easily one of the most beautiful in the world.

Both from Bill Bryson, *Notes from a Small Island*

The second 'Julian' example could have been punctuated with a dash (whereas the first one could not):

The girls wanted to stay – till Julian arrived.

Dashes and brackets make a greater break before an add-on or round an interruption in a sentence than commas do, and are therefore not appropriate for briefer, casual comments like 'by the way', 'you see' and 'after all' that are more closely integrated into the sentence. Dashes and brackets are, however, a useful way of avoiding an excess of commas in a sentence if there are already several commas there for other purposes.

A comma may be used when what follows the comma explains what precedes it:

There are two sorts of people I hate, politicians and spin-doctors.

However, it may be better to use a colon or a dash in this position when a comma might be confusing:

There are two things you need for a good life, status and money.

This does not mean 'For a good life, for status and for money, you need two things' but 'the two things you need for a good life are status and money'. With a colon or dash, this is made clearer:

There are two things you need for a good life: status and money.
There are two things you need for a good life – status and money.

Pauses and breaks

A comma may simply indicate that there should be a pause or break in a sentence, for any of various reasons. There are no hard-and-fast rules about this; it is often a matter of your own judgement. The 'pause test' (see page 80) is often a useful guide.

Pause commas may be added for the sake of clarity, for example when two similar or identical words come together in a sentence:

What they all were, were writers.
One thing Robert wasn't, was a coward.
Those who need to know, know.

. . . or when the final element of the sentence is very short and follows a long, unbroken introductory clause (or clauses):

Galbraith's law states that anyone who says he won't resign four times, will.

J K Galbraith (American economist)

Steven had the sort of friends a child with a mother like she was reputed to be, had.

Isla Dewar, *It Could Happen to You*

. . . or where the latter part of a sentence is not directly linked to what immediately precedes it but to something earlier in the sentence:

Anyone knows that, who knows anything about computers. (= 'anyone who knows . . .')
She believes strongly in the capacity of even those who commit atrocities, to do good. (= '. . . the capacity to do good . . .')

. . . or when two adjacent words or phrases could form a unit, which would mislead the reader:

He worked long hours, for his uncle was a hard task-master. (≠ '. . . worked long hours for his uncle . . .')
What had seemed so daring then, seemed wonderfully innocent now. (≠ '. . . then seemed . . .')

Once you know, the solution is obvious. (≠ 'Once you know the solution . . .')

Optional pauses for emphasis
A pause may serve to emphasize what follows:

I shouted and shouted, but he didn't hear me.
Do you suppose anyone knows if he died, or cares?
I've never had better service in a hotel, or felt more unworthy of it.

Since a comma may indicate a pause that emphasizes something, you often have a choice between inserting and not inserting a comma, depending on the degree of emphasis you want to place on some element of the sentence. Compare the following pairs of examples, and notice how the pauses indicated by the commas in the second version of each pair place greater emphasis on the parts of the sentence they highlight:

Tim did it all by himself.
Tim did it, all by himself.

I had a pain in my leg but eventually it cleared up.
I had a pain in my leg but, eventually, it cleared up.

The boat had a sail as well as an engine.
The boat had a sail, as well as an engine.

If an introductory word or phrase in a sentence is fairly short and unemphatic, there is no need for a comma after it:

Perhaps I'm being too hard on her.

Similarly, linking words and comment words need not be separated off by commas if there is no great emphasis on them:

I'm perhaps being too hard on her.
You are therefore their last hope.
The experience was nevertheless distressing.

But commas indicate more emphasis:

I am, perhaps, being too hard on her.
You are, therefore, their last hope.
The experience was, nevertheless, distressing.

The rule is to follow the rhythm of the sentence and apply the 'pause test' (see page 80).

Alternatives

In a sentence expressing an alternative, there should be no comma between the alternatives.

I want to be a firefighter or a policeman when I grow up.

But when the alternative is an alternative name for something, there should be a comma:

Boyle's original researches were into nitre, or saltpetre. ('nitre' = 'saltpetre')
This rocky island is the home of the gannet, or solan goose. ('gannet' = 'solan goose')

Notice the difference between these two sentences:

Do you want Colin or George to go with you? (= 'or don't you want anyone at all?')

Do you want Colin, or George, to go with you? (= 'one of them is going; choose which one')

Relative clauses

A relative clause is a clause that is linked to a preceding word by a word such as *that, who* or *which*. A relative clause says something about the antecedent:

*Is this the book **that you lent her**?*
*These are the plants **that I was talking about**.*
*He prodded the boy, **who was rigid with terror**.*
*The song thrush, **which was once common**, has disappeared from the UK's top ten species.*

Sometimes there is no linking word:

*Is this the book **you lent her**?*
*These are the plants **I was talking about**.*

There are two types of relative clause and the distinction between them is important because they are punctuated differently.

A relative clause that identifies, picks out or describes a particular person or thing is called a **defining** relative clause. A defining relative clause is not separated off from its antecedent by a comma:

*Have you still got the book **I gave you**?* (This identifies one particular book.)
*You know the man I mean, the man **who drives that old Ford**.* (This identifies one particular man.)
*Who was that fellow **you were talking to**?*
*The book **that was on the table** was mine.*

*She had lost the diamond ring **that I had given her for Christmas***.

*I'll meet you at the spot **where the path crosses the river***.

Relative clauses which do not identify a particular person or thing but simply provide some further information about them are called **non-defining** relative clauses. Non-defining relative clauses *are* separated off from their antecedents, and the rest of the sentence, by commas:

*My neighbours**, who come from Italy,** make wonderful pasta dishes.* (The relative clause does not identify the neighbours but makes a comment about them.)
*'The Hobbit'**, which was written by Tolkien,** is the story of the adventures of Bilbo Baggins.*
*The book**, which was lying beside his bed,** was something to do with UFOs.*
*We met at the bridge**, where we had often met before.***

Errors with the punctuation of defining and non-defining clauses are very common. Note the difference between these examples:

We attached the fuses to the bombs, which were already in place. (= to all the bombs)
We attached the fuses to the bombs which were already in place. (= only to the bombs that were in place, and not to other bombs)
The men, who had attempted to show resistance to the terrorists, were all killed. (= all the men were killed)
The men who had attempted to show resistance to the terrorists were all killed. (= only the men who had resisted were killed)

The following example, with only one comma, is therefore incorrect and ambiguous:

✗ *The men, who had attempted to show resistance to the terrorists were all killed.*

The rule for relative clauses is: always check whether the relative clause is picking out a particular person or thing (in which case there should be no commas round it) or giving additional information as a sort of comment (in which case it should be separated off, as all comments are, by commas).

Summing up

If a relative clause sums up or comments on what has gone before, it should be separated from it by a comma:

The men shared with us what little food they had, which amounted to about a mouthful each.
The girl was very slim and was wearing a tight black dress, which made her seem taller than she actually was.

The presence or absence of a comma may alter the meaning of the sentence:

The girl was very slim and was wearing a tight black dress, which made her seem taller than she actually was. (The tight dress + being slim made her seem taller.)
The girl was very slim and was wearing a tight black dress which made her seem taller than she actually was. (The tight dress made her seem taller.)

Explanations are treated the same way:

I now at last grasped the point of what he had been telling me these past few weeks, that I would need much more money than I had if I was to set up in business on my own.

Without the linking word 'that', there would have to be a colon:

I now at last grasped the point of what he had been telling me these past few weeks: I would need much more money than I had if I was to set up in business on my own.

(See also page 140 for more about the use of colons in elaborations and explanations.)

Apposition

Apposition is the technical name for the grammatical construction in which two nouns or noun phrases referring to the same person or thing stand next to one another in a sentence and the second picks out or provides information about the first. Usually there will be a slight pause at the commas, as is suggested by the commas that must be written round the second element:

*We have had a good response from **you, our members,** to our winter programme of talks.* ('you' = 'our members')
Another grand old man of the theatre, Arthur Morris, *is enjoying a grand old age.* ('grand old man of the theatre' = 'Arthur Morris')

Note that the sentence still makes sense when the word or words within the commas are removed:

We have had a good response from you to our winter programme of talks.

Another grand old man of the theatre is enjoying a grand old age.

In cases like this, it is always wrong to omit the separating commas:

✗ *If you want a hot deal, call me Tom Johnson now for a free estimate.*

✓ *If you want a hot deal, call me, Tom Johnson, now for a free estimate.*

In some cases of apposition, however, the second element is not additional information; the first element is a phrase describing the second element. In this sort of apposition, there should be no commas:

✓ *Grand old man of the theatre Arthur Morris is enjoying a grand old age.*

In this case, the sentence makes sense if the first element is removed, but not when the second element is:

✓ *Arthur Morris is enjoying a grand old age.*
✗ *Grand old man of the theatre is enjoying a grand old age.*

The co-ordinating comma

Co-ordinating commas are inserted between a series of words or phrases that stand together in a sentence and have the same function. For example, there may be a series of descriptive adjectives or adjective phrases:

She spoke in a low, quiet voice.
Today is yet another day of grey, wet, miserable weather.
They are the most beautiful, the most graceful, the most delightful chorus girls in the whole world.

Unloved, unwanted, uncared-for, the children beg in the streets by day and sleep in doorways by night.

. . . or of nouns or noun phrases:

Plates, cups, saucers, bowls – everything crashed to the floor.
Everything was thrown out when we left, all the furniture, all the carpets, all the curtains, all the pictures and ornaments.

. . . or of verbs:

All weekend they measured, sawed, planed, nailed, plastered, painted.
Communism isn't sleeping; it is, as always, plotting, scheming, working, fighting.

Richard Nixon (former US president)

. . . or of adverbs or adverb phrases:

The men worked quietly, confidently, with deadly efficiency.

. . . or of predicates or other phrases:

I have struggled to make something of my life, of my work, of myself.
What are the Conservatives to do? Should they move to the centre, move to the right, push moral values, ignore moral values, be more negative about Labour and the Lib Dems, be more positive about their own policies?

(For commas separating clauses in a sentence, see page 81.)

In sentences like these, you could theoretically replace the commas by 'and' (though in some cases it might make a rather unnatural and stilted sentence):

Today is yet another day of grey and wet and miserable weather.
They are the most beautiful and the most graceful and the most delightful chorus girls in the whole world.
The men worked quietly and confidently and with deadly efficiency.

This is the '*and* test' for commas (see page 81).

If the last two items in a list *are* linked by 'and', there *may* be a comma before the 'and':

The official languages of Singapore are English, Mandarin Chinese, Malay, and Tamil.
They measured, sawed, planed, nailed, plastered, and painted the whole weekend.
Channing was a leading figure in the movement to eliminate slavery, drunkenness, poverty, and war.

. . . but there needn't be:

The official languages of Singapore are English, Mandarin Chinese, Malay and Tamil.
They measured, sawed, planed, nailed, plastered and painted the whole weekend.
We guarantee to rid your lawn of unsightly weeds like daisies, dandelions, clover and speedwell.

The comma inserted before 'and' in this position is often referred to as the 'serial comma' or 'Oxford comma'. While it is optional in British English, it is generally used in American English.

The linking word may be 'or' or 'but' rather than 'and', but the same rule applies:

Always take the mask off when you shower, swim or sleep.
We spent all our time eating, sleeping, sunbathing, or swimming.

She was the selfish, difficult but beautiful daughter of a factory-owner.
We were all very tired, very dirty, but very happy.

When *all* the items in a series are linked by 'and', 'or' or 'but', there should be *no* commas:

Allan was a good and kind man.
They were poor but honest folk.
He sings and dances and plays the piano.
Which do you like best – singing or dancing or playing the piano?

The same is true for words and phrases linked by *either . . . or, neither . . . nor* or *both . . . and*:

Both Nancy and I were delighted.
Neither her sister nor her brothers were invited to the wedding.

Further points to note
• A co-ordinating comma is needed between words that are repeated for emphasis, even though it would be almost impossible to link them with 'and':

That is a wonderful, wonderful idea.
Yes, it's really, really, really annoying.

• The longer the linked elements, the better it is to insert a serial comma:

He raised the bow to his shoulder, took careful aim at the target, and gently released the arrow.
Telling lies is a fault in a boy, an art in a lover, an accomplishment in a bachelor, and second-nature in a married man.

Helen Rowland

(For more on this, see the comments on linking clauses on page 85.)

• There are times when a serial comma, even if optional, is best inserted for the sake of clarity, for example when a series of items includes one which is itself always linked by the word 'and' (for example, the shop 'Marks and Spencer', the composers 'Rodgers and Hammerstein', and food such as 'liver and bacon' and 'salt and vinegar' crisps):

There were various boxes of crisps on the shelf: cheese and onion, tomato, chicken, bacon, salt and vinegar, and beef. (Take out the comma after 'vinegar', and you will see that it would be possible to interpret the last two items as 'salt' and 'vinegar and beef'.)

My favourite foods are sausages, pork pies, and bacon and eggs. Along the coast are Musselburgh, Prestonpans, and Cockenzie and Port Seton. (The comma after 'Prestonpans' shows that the towns are 'Prestonpans' and 'Cockenzie and Port Seton', not 'Prestonpans and Cockenzie' and 'Port Seton'.)

• It is sometimes better *not* to have a serial comma, for example when there is another comma close by marking a stronger break in the sentence:

☒ *I'd have flats in London, Paris, and New York, and a yacht on the Med.*

✓ *I'd have flats in London, Paris and New York, and a yacht on the Med.*

The contrast in this example is between 'flats in London, Paris and New York' and 'a yacht on the Med'. A comma after 'Paris' is undesirable because the comma after 'New York' marks a greater break in the sentence.

- The final item in a series is not followed by a comma:

✗ *I have never read a more ridiculous, pretentious, contrived,*
  piece of nonsense in my life.
✓ *I have never read a more ridiculous, pretentious, contrived*
  piece of nonsense in my life.

An exception to this is when there are two or more phrases or clauses acting as the subject of a sentence:

Her defiant attitude, her refusal to show any sense of shame,
shocked her family but pleased her friends.
What we needed to know, what he had to tell us, was where
they had hidden the bodies.

If the phrases are linked by *and*, however, there are no commas:

Her defiant attitude and her refusal to show any sense of shame
shocked her family but pleased her friends.

- If commas are used to pick out items for the sake of emphasis (see page 99), there must be two commas:

My father had a surprising, but genuine, affection for Kylie.

If there is no particular emphasis, the second comma is not needed:

After our early, amusing, but disastrous attempt to learn to
swim from a book, we decided we had better take proper swim-
ming lessons.

Comma problems with two or more adjectives
- When two adjectives together convey a single idea, they should not be separated by a comma:

good old Peter ('Good' and 'old' together form a single expression of approval or praise.)
a great big dog ('Great' and 'big' form a single expression emphasizing the size of the dog.)

• When two adjectives linked by 'and' form a single unit of meaning, they must not be separated by a comma:

✓ *a big, noisy, red and green bus*
✗ *a big, noisy, red, and green bus* ('Red and green' is a single unit of meaning describing the colour of the bus.)

Sometimes there is unavoidable ambiguity: *red and green buses* could be 'red buses and green buses' or 'buses that are partly red and partly green'.
• If the last of two or more adjectives is more closely linked to the following noun than the other(s), or if it forms a single unit of meaning with the following noun, then it is not preceded by a comma:

✓ *a stupid old man* (= 'an old man who is stupid')
✗ *a stupid, old man*

✓ *a nice front garden* (= 'a front garden that is nice')
✗ *a nice, front garden*

✓ *a red back door* (= 'a back door that is red')
✗ *a red, back door*

Similarly:

a pretty little girl (= 'a little girl who is pretty')
a windy autumn day (= 'an autumn day that is windy')

a dry white wine (= 'a white wine that is dry')
a smelly Italian cheese (= 'an Italian cheese that is smelly')
a lovely old farmhouse (= 'an old farmhouse that is lovely')
a good working knowledge of French (= 'a working knowledge of French that is good')

To check on whether it is appropriate to omit the comma, try the '*and* test': if you would not separate the adjectives with 'and', then don't put in a comma:

✗ *a pretty and little girl*
✗ *a good and working knowledge of French*

You can, of course, put commas between other adjectives:

a cold, wet, windy autumn day
a mild, sweet, fruity white wine
a small, dry, sheltered front garden

The '*and* test' allows this:

a cold and wet and windy autumn day

Among the categories of adjectives that tend not to be separated off by commas are adjectives denoting materials (*wooden, plastic, iron,* etc), adjectives denoting a place of origin (*French, Italian, American,* etc), and adjectives denoting dates (e.g. *16th-century*):

an 18th-century Italian iron bucket

• It is now common practice to omit commas between two adjectives describing a following noun, although it is still correct to put in the commas if they pass the '*and* test':

✓ *Along the road came a big red bus.*
✓ *Along the road came a big, red bus.*

✓ *We all had to wear long scratchy underwear.*
✓ *We all had to wear long, scratchy underwear.*

With three or more adjectives describing what something is like, it is normal to put in commas:

Along the road came a big, red, noisy bus.
She gave him a long, hard, cold look.
We all had to wear long, scratchy, knitted underwear.

However, as noted above, there are certain categories of adjectives that tend not to be separated off by commas, such as adjectives denoting materials, origins and dates. Another category to include here is adjectives giving an opinion (*great, lovely, excellent*, etc), which tend to come at the beginning of a series of adjectives:

a lovely orange sunset
The BBC provides some excellent educational programmes

In series of or including adjectives in these categories, there are therefore usually no commas:

Someone I know once stole a lovely big yellow plastic duck from a shop.
She served up some ghastly vinegary Greek wine.
Dexter was an eccentric 18th-century American merchant.

Sometimes the difference in meaning indicated by the presence or absence of a comma is very slight. Don't agonize too much over this. Apply the '*and* test', and also the 'pause test' (see page 80):

a lovely refreshing drink (= 'a refreshing drink that is lovely')
a lovely, refreshing drink (= 'a drink that is both lovely and refreshing')

some excellent educational programmes (= 'educational programmes that are excellent, as opposed to ones that are not very good')
some excellent, educational programmes (= 'programmes that are both excellent and educational')

When adjectives are preceded by words like *very, extremely, rather, quite,* etc, put in the commas:

Along the road came a very big, very noisy bus.

. . . although in many such cases you might more naturally link the adjective phrases with 'and', in which case there would be no need for a comma:

Along the road came a very big and very noisy bus.

• The absence of a comma between two adjectives is now so well established that one can no longer argue against it. However, you should be aware that the presence or absence of a comma between two adjectives can sometimes imply a slight, and often quite subtle, difference in meaning. Consider these two examples:

James bought a new, red car.
James bought a new red car.

The first example implies that James has bought a new car which just happens to be red. The second example, on the other hand, implies something slightly different:

James already had a red car and has now bought another red car.

But of course, now that it has become common practice not to put a comma in between two adjectives in this position, this distinction is lost: *James bought a new red car* could have either meaning.

In a similar vein, compare these two examples:

Officers from the Bomb Squad were called out to investigate a suspicious object in a small, white van parked outside the bank. (The van just happened to be both small and white.)
Two white vans were stolen, a large one and a small one. The police have found the large white van but are still looking for the small white van. (Of the two white vans, they have found the large one but not the small one.)

And again:

Should I wear my black, leather gloves or my brown, woollen ones? (gloves that are black and leather or gloves that are brown and woollen)
Should I wear my black leather gloves or my brown leather gloves? (leather gloves that are black or leather gloves that are brown)

In all such cases, the distinction would be indicated in speech by a difference in the stress patterns of the sentences; for example:

Should I wear my black, leather *gloves or my brown,* woollen *ones?*
Should I wear my black *leather gloves or my* brown *leather gloves?*

Here are two further examples:

The revised paperback edition of Jones's book is out now. (= 'a revised version of the already existing paperback edition')

The revised, paperback edition of Jones's book is out now. (= 'a revised version of a non-paperback book; the revised edition is being published as a paperback')

Have you any other young singers on your books? (= 'talking about young singers, have you any others?')

Have you any other, young singers on your books? (='talking about singers, have you any others who are young?')

The balancing comma

A comma is used where there is a balance or contrast in a sentence with repeated or similar elements:

The more she cried, the more he hated her.
The harder the climb, the greater the satisfaction when you reach the top.
Nothing ventured, nothing gained.
So little done, so much to do.

Cecil Rhodes

From each according to his abilities, to each according to his needs.

Karl Marx

It is, however, correct to write short balanced phrases without commas, especially when there is another comma nearby marking a stronger break:

I'll see how it goes, but so far so good.
My brother liked his girlfriends to be totally crazy, the wilder the better.

A stronger balance or contrast must be punctuated with a semicolon:

Brigands demand your money or your life; women require both.

(Attributed to) Samuel Butler

In particular, when the balance is between two sentences already punctuated with commas, the two should be separated by a semicolon:

Those who can, do; those who can't, teach.

George Bernard Shaw

The comma of omission

When a word is omitted from a sentence, its place is often marked by a comma:

Éclairs are strange cakes – one minute they're there, the next, they're gone, just like that. (= '. . . the next minute . . .')

When a comma is used to indicate an omission in part of the sentence, it is often better to mark a balance between two parts with a semicolon rather than another comma:

To err is human; to forgive, divine.

Sometimes no comma is required to show an omission:

He loved her, and she him. (= '. . . and she loved him')

In fact, if the only other punctuation mark in the sentence is a comma, or if there is no other punctuation mark, it is wrong to use a comma to mark an omission:

✗ *He loved her, and she, him.*
✗ *He loved her and she, him.*

Here again, as in so many other instances, the need for a comma is often indicated by a slight pause. Use the 'pause test' (see page 80).

Too many commas can be confusing. A sentence like the following would be considered acceptable by some authorities on punctuation:

☒ *Paris is famous for its galleries and museums, Rome, for its piazzas and fountains, and London, for its pageantry and nightlife.*

Personally, I would not accept this as good style: there are too many commas. Either the omission commas should be removed or the balancing commas should be upgraded to semicolons:

✓ *Paris is famous for its galleries and museums, Rome for its piazzas and fountains, and London for its pageantry and nightlife.*
✓ *Paris is famous for its galleries and museums; Rome, for its piazzas and fountains; and London, for its pageantry and nightlife.*

Lastly, notice that if you omit the word 'that' in a sentence, you do *not* mark the omission with a comma:

I said that I was coming.
✓ *I said I was coming.*
✗ *I said, I was coming.*

Knock-on effects

Sometimes the presence of one punctuation mark in a sentence may lead you to insert, omit or change another elsewhere in the sentence. For example, it is acceptable to write a short balanced sentence such as *The sooner, the better* with or without a comma. However, if such a phrase appears in a longer sentence where there is another nearby comma marking a stronger break, it may be better to omit the balancing comma:

✗ *I like chillies, the hotter, the better.*
✓ *I like chillies, the hotter the better.*

Alternatively, you could replace the first comma with a dash and keep the second one:

✓ *I like chillies – the hotter, the better.*

Again, compare the punctuation in these sentences:

Gran gave the sweets to Joan and Pat was very upset.
Gran gave the sweets to Joan and Pat, seeing this, was very upset.

With 'seeing this' interrupting the sentence, the words 'Gran gave the sweets to Joan and Pat' could be misinterpreted. To avoid this, a comma must be inserted after 'Joan' to show the correct structure and meaning of the sentence:

✗ *Gran gave the sweets to Joan and Pat, seeing this, was very upset.*
✓ *Gran gave the sweets to Joan, and Pat, seeing this, was very upset.*

There are many instances of this sort of thing. They are yet another part of punctuation that must be handled by a commonsense principle and personal judgement rather than by rule, since there is no hard-and-fast rule that could cover them all. The principle is simple: if something could be misinterpreted as it stands, punctuate it to make the meaning clear. And if punctuation doesn't do the trick, rewrite the sentence.

Commas for full stops

Look out also for sentence strings (see page 38), with commas where there should be full stops.

Structure versus pauses: a grey area

If you look at the following example, you can see that there is an interruption (see page 93), 'where necessary', in it. The interruption is separated off, as you would expect, by two commas:

Our methods are regularly reviewed and, where necessary, are updated to ensure best practice is followed.

Notice that if 'where necessary' is removed, the sentence still makes sense:

✓ *Our methods are regularly reviewed and are updated to ensure best practice is followed.*

Whether or not a sentence would still make sense when an interruption like this is removed is generally taken to be the key to the correct placement of commas: commas should go round the words that would still leave a meaningful sentence if they were removed. As a rule, this works, and it should be adopted as a general principle.

The commas often correspond to slight pauses in the sentence:

Our methods are regularly reviewed and, ↓ where necessary, ↓ are updated to ensure best practice is followed.

When pauses correspond to breaks in the structure of a sentence, there is no problem with punctuation. However, many people would naturally say the sentence with pauses after 'reviewed' not after 'and':

Our methods are regularly reviewed ↓ and where necessary ↓ are updated to ensure best practice is followed.

Following the *rhythm* of the sentence, therefore, they might want to punctuate it as follows:

Our methods are regularly reviewed, and where necessary, are updated to ensure best practice is followed.

. . . even though the sentence would make no sense if the part between the commas was removed:

✗ *Our methods are regularly reviewed are updated to ensure best practice is followed.*

There is often this sort of clash between the logical structure of a sentence and its natural rhythm. Another example is this one from Partridge (*You Have a Point There*):

I don't like suggesting this, but if it's at all possible, I should be grateful for your help.

If you say this sentence, it is clear that you would naturally make slight pauses at the points indicated by the commas. But here again, if you take out the part of the sentence between the commas, the sentence no longer makes sense:

✗ *I don't like suggesting this I should be grateful for your help.*

What are you to do, then, when the rhythm of the sentence leads you to punctuate it in one way, while the structure of the sentence leads you to punctuate it in another way? Authorities disagree. Some argue that you should *always* follow logic and punctuate according to the structure of the sentence:

Our methods are regularly reviewed and, where necessary, are updated to ensure best practice is followed.
I don't like suggesting this but, if it's at all possible, I should be grateful for your help.

Others (and Partridge is among them, as were the Fowlers in *The King's English*) argue that you should ignore the structure and follow the *rhythm* of the sentence:

Our methods are regularly reviewed, and where necessary, are updated to ensure best practice is followed.
I don't like suggesting this, but if it's at all possible, I should be grateful for your help.

It is generally agreed that punctuation that follows both structure *and* rhythm is over-punctuation:

☒ *I don't like suggesting this, but, if it's at all possible, I should be grateful for your help.*

If you have to choose between structure and rhythm, a rhythm-based punctuation is probably the better option because it reflects natural speech. There are examples in this book:

You can, of course, decide not to punctuate sentences with capital letters and full stops, **but if you do,** *you will be breaking two of the fixed rules of English punctuation.*
Now, this is a perfectly valid definition of a sentence, **and if you apply it to any page in a book, magazine or newspaper,** *you will easily pick out all the sentences.*

A grammar-based punctuation would have required the following:

You can, of course, decide not to punctuate sentences with capital letters and full stops **but,** **if** *you do, you will be breaking two of the fixed rules of English punctuation.*
Now, this is a perfectly valid definition of a sentence **and,** **if** *you apply it to any page in a book, magazine or newspaper, you will easily pick out all the sentences.*

If you do adopt the rhythm-based approach to punctuation, be prepared for other people to disagree with your decision (perhaps quite strongly), but don't let them persuade you that you are wrong.

Summary of key points

- Do not add commas to sentences needlessly. Many sentences do not require commas at all. Always check your work and remove unnecessary punctuation.

- A subordinate clause is frequently separated from a following main clause by a comma, though it is not always necessary to do so. When in doubt, put a comma in.

- A subordinate clause whose only verb is a participle should be separated from a preceding or following clause by a comma.

- Main clauses linked by words such as *and* or *but* are not separated by a comma if they have the same subject or deal with a single topic. But with different subjects and unconnected or contrasting topics, there should be a comma between the clauses.

- *And, but, or, so, while* and *yet* can be preceded by a comma; other connecting words (such as *consequently, for example, however, instead, moreover* and *nevertheless*) must be preceded by a semicolon. Particular care should be taken with *however*.

- Three or more main clauses can be separated by commas; if there are only two clauses, they are usually separated by a semicolon, unless there is a linking word between them, in which case a comma is correct.

- Comments, names, exclamations, etc are separated off from the rest of the sentence by commas.

- Commas may be used to mark pauses, for emphasis and clarity.
- Commas are required round non-defining relative clauses, but not round defining relative clauses.
- Commas are required in lists of words or phrases having the same function in a sentence.
- Commas are required between short balanced phrases; longer balanced elements require semicolons.
- Commas may indicate the omission of a word or phrase.
- When structure and rhythm suggest different punctuation, follow rhythm.

Position of commas with parentheses and quotation marks

A comma should follow the closing bracket of a preceding parenthetical comment:

Since I had not yet learned the basic facts of life (which were something my parents didn't think I needed to know), I had some very odd notions about storks, rhubarb bushes and babies.

The comma does not precede the comment, nor should there be two commas:

✗ *Since I had not yet learned the basic facts of life, (which were something my parents didn't think I needed to know) I had some very odd notions about storks, rhubarb bushes and babies.*

✗ *Since I had not yet learned the basic facts of life, (which were something my parents didn't think I needed to know),*

I had some very odd notions about storks, rhubarb bushes and babies.

With quotation marks, for example round highlighted words, the comma should follow the closing quotation mark:

The focus of such a life is always 'me', my thoughts, my needs, my experiences.

Notice that American practice differs from British practice, just as it does with the full stop (see page 46):

The focus of such a life is always "me," my thoughts, my needs, my experiences.

Commas in direct speech
A comma replaces a full stop at the end of a sentence in direct speech:

'That looks very tasty,' said James.

When a sentence in direct speech is split by a verb of speaking, the split in the sentence is marked with a comma. The comma is usually placed inside the closing quotation mark:

'I must tell you,' he said, 'what happened this afternoon.'
'There are,' she said, 'a lot of changes to be made round here.'

However, there are some people who argue (quite logically) that when a comma is not part of the sentence of direct speech, it should go outside the quotation marks, and only be placed inside the closing quotation mark when it belongs to the original sentence. Compare the following examples:

'I must tell you', he said, *'what happened this afternoon.'*
(The sentence of direct speech is *I must tell you what happened this afternoon*, with no comma, so the comma indicating the split in the sentence goes outside the quotation marks.)
'I must tell you, John,' he said, 'what happened this afternoon.'
(The sentence of direct speech is *I must tell you, John, what happened this afternoon*, with a comma after *John*, so the comma indicating the split in the sentence goes inside the quotation marks.)

'There are', she said, *'a lot of changes to be made round here.'*
(The sentence of direct speech is *There are a lot of changes to be made round here*, with no comma, so the comma indicating the split in the sentence goes outside the quotation marks.)
'There are, boys,' she said, 'a lot of changes to be made round here.'
(The sentence of direct speech is *There are, boys, a lot of changes to be made round here*, with a comma after *boys*, so the comma indicating the split in the sentence goes inside the quotation marks.)

While this is an entirely logical and commendable rule, it is not the rule that most people currently accept and apply. It is more in keeping with current practice always to put the comma inside the closing quotation mark at a split.

Note that there is also a comma after the verb of speaking when it splits a sentence:

'I must tell you,' he said, 'what happened this afternoon.'
'There are,' she said, 'a lot of changes to be made round here.'

But when what follows the verb is a new sentence, there is a full stop:

'There are a lot of changes to be made round here,' she said.
'We'll start tomorrow.'

Other punctuation marks in direct speech are neither replaced by nor accompanied by a comma:

'What was that noise?' she whispered.
'Look out!' he shouted.

When a speech verb precedes direct speech, it is generally followed by a comma:

She turned to him and said, 'I hate you.'
My Mum gave me a look that said, don't argue with me.
I must have told you boys a hundred times, don't leave your bags in the corridor.

(Note that direct speech need not always be enclosed in quotation marks; see page 170.)

The comma may be omitted, but it is still normal practice to put one in. Some people use a colon instead of the comma:

She turned to him and said: 'I hate you.'

The comma is preferable, however, as colons usually mark stronger sentence breaks than are required before direct speech.

Commas in numbers

There are no commas in two- or three-figure numbers:

37
202

With four-figure numbers, a comma is optional but in

keeping with the tendency towards less punctuation, it is probably better now to omit it:

3521 or *3,521*

With numbers of five or more figures, there should be a comma marking off every group of three figures, counting from the units:

37,451,521

Sometimes in printing, thin spaces are used instead of commas.

There are no commas in numbers after a decimal point:

37.134756067

Commas may be used in dates, but here again the current tendency is to omit them:

He was born on 4 February, 1949.
He was born on 4 February 1949.
I think it was in August, 1973, that I first went to London.
I think it was in August 1973 that I first went to London.

There should be a comma between the day of the month and the year if they are juxtaposed:

On February 4, 1949, a singular event took place: my birth.

Commas in letters and addresses
See page 261.

8
Semicolons

Sometimes you get a glimpse of a semicolon coming, a few lines farther on, and it is like climbing a steep path through woods and seeing a wooden bench just at a bend in the road ahead, a place where you can expect to sit for a moment, catching your breath.

Lewis Thomas

A semicolon makes a break in a sentence that is stronger than one made by a comma but weaker than one marked by a full stop. In fact, semicolons are most often used in place of commas or full stops where these two punctuation marks would for some reason not be appropriate. It will be helpful, therefore, to discuss the semicolon from that point of view.

Semicolon instead of full stop
A semicolon is used to link passages of writing that *could* be written as separate sentences but which a writer feels are so closely connected in sense or theme that a full stop would make too strong a break between them. The semicolon lessens the break. For example, one could write the following three separate sentences,

each grammatically complete in itself, to describe the ending of a play:

The curtain is down. The players have left the stage. Our play is ended.

But as these three sentences together relate to a single event (the end of the play), a writer wanting to show the close connection between them might feel that the breaks created by the full stops were too strong. To lessen the breaks while still keeping the sentences to some extent separate, it would be correct to use semicolons instead of the full stops, so forming the sentences into a larger unit, a 'super-sentence' (see page 33):

The curtain is down; the players have left the stage; our play is ended.

When to link sentences together in super-sentences is not something that can be learnt by rule; it must always be a matter of personal judgement in a particular context. But some further examples may illustrate the principle:

The war ended; a treaty was signed; trade between the two kingdoms began again. (This is a series of linked events following one after the other.)
Dulcie's hair and make-up were striking; her jewellery was modern and ostentatious; her dress was designer-labelled and expensive. (All three sentences are closely linked, in that they are describing a person's appearance.)
An old woman was shooing away a crowd of naked children; evidently there was something that the children ought not to

see. (The old woman was shooing the children away *because* there was something they ought not to see.)

If it is a mile from the pit bottom to the coal face, that is probably an average distance; three miles is a fairly normal one; there are even said to be a few mines where it is as much as five miles.

George Orwell, *The Road to Wigan Pier*

(All three sentences are commenting on the distances miners have to walk to the coal face.)

In the last example, there is an element of contrast between the three sentences: a mile – three miles – five miles. Semicolons are often used in this way to link sentences in which there is a balance or contrast:

Some of the peasants hardly seemed to care about the squalor in the village; others clearly understood the misery they were living in.

All I was risking was captivity; they were risking their lives.

'Only another four hundred feet to the top,' he said encouragingly; he might as well have said another four hundred miles.

Growing old is unavoidable; growing up is optional.

Capitalism is the exploitation of one man by another; communism is the other way round.

The Cold War isn't thawing; it is burning with a deadly heat. Communism isn't sleeping; it is, as always, plotting, scheming, working, fighting.

Richard Nixon (former US president)

The power which establishes a state is violence; the power which maintains it is violence; the power which eventually overthrows it is violence.

Kenneth Kaunda (former president of Zambia)

Even with incomplete sentences, colons are used to mark balances and contrasts:

If you want to be happy for a short time, get drunk; happy for a long time, fall in love; happy for ever, take up gardening.

Arthur Smith

Semicolon instead of comma
• When contrasting or balanced clauses are linked by a conjunction, they are usually punctuated by a comma:

He may be sick as a parrot, but I'm over the moon.
Although we like Tony as a person, we dislike him as a politician.

Without the conjunction, the balanced or contrasting elements become separate sentences, and so a semi-colon is the punctuation mark to use:

He may be sick as a parrot; I'm over the moon.
We like Tony as a person; we dislike him as a politician.

Even with a conjunction such as *and, but, for, or, nor, so, while* and *yet* (usually preceded by a comma), the comma may be replaced by a semicolon to make a greater break in the sentence (generally corresponding to a pause), and so more strongly emphasize what follows:

The letter had been returned unopened; and unopened it had remained ever since.
This time we got what we needed; but only after a lot of telephoning.
How Victorian her behaviour was at times, I thought; but then, how Victorian her upbringing had been in some respects.
It was lucky that someone saw Paul being taken away by the

secret police; otherwise we would have had no idea what had happened to him.

• A comma may be used without a linking word where there is a balance or contrast between sentences with repeated or similar elements:

Nothing ventured, nothing gained.
The more she cried, the more he hated her.
The more often she asks for a pay rise, the less likely she is to get one.

However, when the contrasting or balanced elements themselves contain one or more commas (for example separating clauses or indicating omitted words (see page 117), the split between the balanced or contrasting elements should be punctuated by a semicolon:

✗ *If your lawn requires treatment for moss and weeds, we will carry it out, if it doesn't, we won't.*
✓ *If your lawn requires treatment for moss and weeds, we will carry it out; if it doesn't, we won't.*
✗ *In France we bought cardigans, in England, shoes, in Ireland, whiskey.*
✓ *In France we bought cardigans; in England, shoes; in Ireland, whiskey.*

(For an alternative punctuation, see page 118.)

Semicolons should be used instead of commas in any sentence where an excess of commas might be confusing or misleading. Semicolons group items clearly where commas might not:

Instead of getting down to discussing business, they had dis-cussed the government's proposal to introduce identity cards;

the American election; Miss Park's pet poodle which, by the sound of it, was not long for this world; the film she had gone to see the previous evening, which she had not enjoyed; the book Man and Boy, *which she was reading in bed; the various illnesses her family and friends were suffering from, and her proposed remedies; the trip to Barcelona she was planning for the summer, and the Gaudí cathedral, which she was dying to see; and the lack of facilities in the Barnton, the hotel she was staying in while in town.*

• Semicolons should be used in a 'super-sentence' in which there is a mixture of structures in parallel, some being sentences (that could be punctuated with full stops) but others less than sentences (that could in theory be separated by commas):

I thought about approaching her when she came out of her office, in order to explain what had happened, but I rejected that idea; thought about writing to her, but rejected that idea too; considered a huge bunch of flowers; a small gift; an expensive gift; my undying love; my abject apologies; none of these seemed quite right.

• Some linking words (such as *also, consequently, for example, furthermore, hence, however, instead, moreover, nevertheless, therefore* and *thus*) must be preceded by a semicolon rather than a comma, and are usually followed by a comma:

The boiler broke down; consequently, the school was closed for two days.
All forms of the media affect us; moreover, they often affect us in ways we are not aware of.

Your privacy is important to us; therefore, we will never sell or give your personal details to any other company.

• A series of three or more short sentences may be separated by commas:

I was thick, I was fat, I was useless at games, I wore old patched clothes, I smelt. No wonder I was unpopular at school.

However, two sentences should be separated by a semicolon:

We were all hungry; some of us were exhausted as well.

You can, however, use a comma between two closely related and balanced parts of a sentence when the first one has a negative word (such as *not*) in it and the second one is a comment on the first:

He wasn't just tipsy, he was legless.

Semicolon or colon?
• Like semicolons, colons may be used in sentences where one part is balanced against the other:

On the Continent people have good food: in England people have good table manners.

George Mikes

This often happens in traditional proverbs and pithy sayings:

To err is human: to forgive, divine.

However, nowadays a semicolon is preferred in balanced sayings of this type:

To err is human; to forgive, divine.

. . . but a colon is used to make a strong contrast:

God is love: man is hate.

When there is a linking word between the contrasting elements, a semicolon or a comma should be used:

Man proposes; but God disposes.
Man proposes, but God disposes.

• In introducing lists, a colon is used when *all* the options are specified, whereas a semicolon is used when only *some* of the possible options are mentioned:

The Gauls were afraid of only one thing: that the sky might fall on their heads.
I'm afraid of lots of things; of dogs, of the dark, of bogeymen under the bed, of being alone, of flying, of dying.

But if a complete list of options is introduced by *namely* or *that is*, a semicolon may be used instead of a colon:

The Gauls were afraid of only one thing; namely, that the sky might fall on their heads.

Other acceptable ways of punctuating sentences with *namely*, etc are:

The Gauls were afraid of only one thing: namely, that the sky might fall on their heads.
The Gauls were afraid of only one thing – namely, that the sky might fall on their heads.
The Gauls were afraid of only one thing, namely that the sky might fall on their heads.

Semicolon, colon or full stop?

Sentences punctuated with full stops simply state facts with no connection between them:

George Bush has been elected President. Thousands of Americans have left for a new life in Canada.

Punctuation with a semicolon would suggest a closer link between the happenings described. Perhaps they took place at the same time, for example, and might be mentioned in a list of recent happenings in America:

George Bush has been elected President; thousands of Americans have left for a new life in Canada; the dollar has fallen against the euro.

Punctuation with a colon, however, suggests a much closer link between the two happenings, i.e. cause and effect:

George Bush has been elected President: thousands of Americans have left for a new life in Canada.

With the colon, it is clearly being stated that the Americans have gone to Canada *because* George Bush has been elected.

Comma for semicolon in a quotation

A comma replaces a semicolon when a quotation is interrupted by a speech verb:

As Samuel Johnson said: 'I will be conquered; I will not capitulate.'
'I will be conquered,' as Samuel Johnson said, 'I will not capitulate.'

American English

Unlike full stops and commas (see pages 46 and 126), semicolons are placed *outside* closing quotation marks in American English:

He called himself a "horse whisperer"; he could read a horse's mind.

Summary of key points

- A semicolon makes a break in a sentence that is stronger than one made by a comma but weaker than one marked by a full stop. A semicolon is therefore used to lessen the break between sentences that could be punctuated with full stops, and to increase the break between parts of sentences that could be punctuated with commas.
- Semicolons are used instead of full stops in a series of closely related sentences.
- Semicolons are used in sentences with balanced or contrasting elements.
- Semicolons are used to avoid a confusing excess of commas.

9
Colons

Anyone who puts a colon in a letter is immediately suspect.

Marjorie Proops

Careful punctuation, it seems, is not the strong point of those who write for agony columns. The agony aunt Marjorie Proops once said that she always considered suspect any letter she received that had a colon in it: it was probably a hoax.

However, even if you might be better to avoid using colons should you ever write to an agony column, you should not neglect them in other contexts. The colon is an important punctuation mark, with a range of uses that cannot correctly be performed by any other punctuation mark.

The colon introducing explanations and descriptions
A colon is used to introduce a part of a sentence that explains, completes or elaborates on what has gone before:

2004 is quite a milestone for us: the Association is 25 years old.
(2004 is a milestone *because* the Association is 25 years old.)

The programme was inspired by an increasingly common TV assumption: war is the only part of history to matter. (That war is the only part of history that matters *is* the assumption.)
One thing was obvious: the man was exhausted.
I can sometimes forget about her for a few hours at a time, and then it will suddenly hit me again: life without her will be unbearable.
Her basic problem is this: she believes she is both unloved and unlovable.

Using the 'pause test' (see page 80), you will probably find that you will pause slightly at the point where the colon goes.

A similar use of the colon to expand on something is seen in the following example, in which the second part elaborates on what was mentioned in the first part by insisting on it:

You can do it: and you will!

In less formal writing, a dash could be used instead of a colon:

One thing was obvious – the man was exhausted.
You can do it – and you will!

Do not use a colon if the two parts of the sentence are already linked in some other way:

✓ *Her basic problem is this: she believes she is both unloved and unlovable.*
✗ *Her basic problem is that: she believes she is both unloved and unlovable.* (There should be no colon because the link is made by 'is that'.)

✓ *Her basic problem is that she believes she is both unloved and unlovable.*

✓ *I know why the sun never sets on the British Empire: God wouldn't trust an Englishman in the dark.*

Duncan Spaeth

✗ *The sun never sets on the British Empire because: God wouldn't trust an Englishman in the dark.* (There should be no colon because a link is already being made by 'because'.)
✓ *The sun never sets on the British Empire because God wouldn't trust an Englishman in the dark.*

Do not use a semicolon or a comma to link two parts of a sentence of this type:

✗ *This is how right-wing this guy is; he thinks George Bush isn't right-wing enough.*
✓ *This is how right-wing this guy is: he thinks George Bush isn't right-wing enough.*

✗ *The cause of last weekend's rail crash must await the outcome of an official inquiry, but one thing is clear, we need a full-time Transport Secretary instead of one who also acts as Scottish Secretary.*
✓ *The cause of last weekend's rail crash must await the outcome of an official inquiry, but one thing is clear: we need a full-time Transport Secretary instead of one who also acts as Scottish Secretary.*

A comma is permissible at a weaker break with a linking word:

I now at last grasped the point of what he had been telling me these past few weeks, that I would need much more money than I had if I was to set up in business on my own.

Without the linking word 'that', there would have to be a colon:

I now at last grasped the point of what he had been telling me these past few weeks: I would need much more money than I had if I was to set up in business on my own.

Colon, full stop or semicolon?

When statements are punctuated with full stops, they simply state facts:

Will the series get across what makes the community tick? From what we saw in the first programme, I doubt it. We don't really get to know much about any of the people who live there.

A colon, on the other hand, shows that there is a cause-and-effect relationship between adjacent statements:

Will the series get across what makes the community tick? From what we saw in the first programme, I doubt it: we don't really get to know much about any of the people there.

The colon in the second version of the paragraph emphasizes *why* the writer has his doubts: it is *because* you don't get to know the people properly.

A colon between two statements makes a closer connection between them than a semicolon does, but often there is little difference in meaning or effect:

We have two dogs; one is a spaniel and the other is a collie. (two bare facts)

We have two dogs: one is a spaniel and the other is a collie.
(the second statement specifically elaborates on the first)

However, for an example showing important meaning implications of choosing between a full stop, a semicolon and a colon, see page 138.

The colon introducing definitions

A colon may be used to introduce a definition. This is simply a particular case of what precedes the colon being explained by what follows it:

Alimony: bounty after the mutiny.

Max Kauffmann

Desertion: an aversion to fighting as exhibited by abandoning an army or a wife.

Ambrose Bierce

The colon introducing descriptions

Colons can be used in descriptions in which what follows the colon describes or elaborates on what precedes the colon:

The wide valley spread out below me: broad fields, dark woodlands, little villages linked by narrow winding roads.
Suddenly it was spring again: the woods became alive with the singing of the birds; the hills and meadows were covered with wild flowers; and everywhere you looked there were people working in the fields.

The second example could have had a semicolon in place of the colon:

Suddenly it was spring again; the woods became alive with the singing of the birds; the hills and meadows were covered with wild flowers; and everywhere you looked there were people working in the fields.

A semicolon would, however, lessen the link between the sentences, reducing them to four simple statements of fact. What the colon does is emphasize a causal relationship: it was *because* it was spring that the birds were singing, the flowers were in bloom and people were working in the fields.

The colon introducing lists

A colon is used to introduce a list:

Since bird-watching is an outdoor activity, it is recommended that you have the following things with you: a water bottle, a map, all-weather clothing, towels, gloves, a torch, plastic bags for rubbish, and insect repellent.

If the items listed are long, they can be set apart on separate lines:

To assess your claim, we need the following things:
    your fully filled-in claim form
    a copy of your financial assessment
    proof of all other income and savings
    proof of your rent
    proof of your identity

The rules for visitors are as follows:
    1) You can only stay in the UK for 6 months.
    2) You will not be permitted to work whilst in the UK.
    3) You must not intend to study.

4) *You must have adequate accommodation.*
5) *You must have the finances to support yourself for the duration of your stay.*
6) *You must be able to meet the cost of your onward journey.*

The matters to be discussed are:
 (a) print run
 (b) price
 (c) jacket
 (d) publication date
 (e) marketing strategy

Notice that in this last example the colon interrupts the structure of the sentence:

The matters to be discussed are print run, price, . . .

This is only permitted with a list of items on separate lines or in some way separated off from one another:

✓ *The matters to be discussed are: (a) print run; (b) price; . . .*
✗ *The matters to be discussed are: print run, price, . . .*
✓ *The matters to be discussed are print run, price, . . .*

Whether the colon should be, or even may be, followed by a dash when introducing a list is a matter of disagreement among authorities. For some, the answer is 'never, never, never'. Others suggest that there should be no dash when the listed items immediately follow the colon on the same line, but that a dash is acceptable (though not necessary) when the listed items begin on a new line. That is the position adopted in this book:

✗ *Since bird-watching is an outdoor activity, it is recommended that you have the following things with you:– a water bottle, a map, all-weather clothing, towels, gloves, a torch, plastic bags for rubbish, and insect repellent.*

✓ *To assess your claim, we need the following things:–*
   your fully filled-in claim form
   a copy of your financial assessment
   proof of all other income and savings
   proof of your rent
   proof of your identity

. . . or equally well:

✓ *To assess your claim, we need the following things:*
   your fully filled-in claim form
   a copy of . . .

Do not use a hyphen, though; always a dash.

There should, of course, be no colon at all when the link is already made in some other way in a sentence:

✗ *Applicants should have GCSE passes in: English, maths, a science and a language.*
✓ *Applicants should have GCSE passes in English, maths, a science and a language.*
✓ *Applicants should have GCSE passes in the following subjects: English, maths, a science and a language.*

Colon or semicolon?

In introducing lists, use a colon when *all* the options are specified, but a semicolon when only *some* of the possible options are mentioned:

The Gauls were afraid of only one thing: that the sky might fall on their heads.

I'm afraid of lots of things; of dogs, of the dark, of bogeymen under the bed, of being alone, of flying, of dying.

But when a list of options is introduced by *namely* or *that is*, there are various ways of introducing the options:

The Gauls were afraid of only one thing: namely, that the sky might fall on their heads.
The Gauls were afraid of only one thing; namely, that the sky might fall on their heads.
The Gauls were afraid of only one thing, namely that the sky might fall on their heads.
The Gauls were afraid of only one thing – namely, that the sky might fall on their heads.

The dash is, as always, more informal than the other options.

The colon introducing a summing-up
A colon may be used to introduce a part of a sentence that sums up what has gone before:

Good food, good wine, good books, good music, good friends: these are the things that make life tolerable.

More informally, this could be done with a dash:

Good food, good wine, good books, good music, good friends – these are the things that make life tolerable.

The colon introducing direct speech and quotations

A colon may be used before direct speech:

She repeatedly mouthed: 'Thank you, thank you.'
All she could do was say with resignation in her voice: 'I am sure you did your best, my dear.'

A colon makes a rather emphatic introduction to speech and is mostly used in formal, solemn or dramatic contexts. Nowadays a comma is normally used in general contexts of informal conversation, as in novels:

He glanced up at her and said, 'You look fantastic.'
Barry commented, 'If all you pay is peanuts, then all you'll get is monkeys.'

Colons are frequently used to introduce speech in plays, as in this excerpt from Tom Stoppard's *Rosencrantz and Guildenstern Are Dead*:

GUIL: Then what are we doing here, I ask myself.
ROS: You might well ask.
GUIL: We better get on.
ROS: You might well think.
GUIL: We better get on.

A colon is correctly used before longer, weightier quotations:

Martin had written down a quotation he thought Jane would like: 'We are the music-makers, and we are the dreamers of dreams.'

. . . and *must* be used if the quotation begins on a new line:

As Shelley once wrote:
  The seed ye sow, another reaps;
  The wealth ye find, another keeps;
  The robes ye weave, another wears;
  The arms ye forge, another bears.

When direct speech or a quotation stands in the middle of a sentence, there should be no colon or comma to disrupt the structure of the sentence:

✗ *As the result was announced, she screamed: 'Oh, my God' and began to shake. (= '. . . she screamed and began to shake')*

✓ *As the result was announced, she screamed 'Oh, my God' and began to shake.*

✗ *For some reason the old adage: 'Be careful what you wish for' springs to mind. (= '. . . the old adage springs to mind')*

✓ *For some reason the old adage 'Be careful what you wish for' springs to mind.*

Colons for balance and contrast
• Like semicolons, colons may be used in sentences where one part is balanced against or contrasted with the other:

To err is human: to forgive, divine.
On the Continent people have good food: in England people have good table manners.

George Mikes

However, nowadays a semicolon is preferred:

To err is human; to forgive, divine.

. . . but a colon is used to emphasize a strong contrast between the two, usually short, contrasting elements:

Man proposes: God disposes.

When there is a linking word between the contrasting elements, a semicolon or a comma should be used:

Man proposes; but God disposes.
Man proposes, but God disposes.

. . . unless a strong contrast is wanted, in which case the colon can be used along with a conjunction:

He died young: but he died happy.

• In narrative, colons may be used instead of full stops or semicolons as a dramatic device to produce a staccato effect when describing two or more actions. Examples are not common; these are taken from *The Oxford Companion to the English Language*:

I called: you did not answer.
He arrived: he knocked on the door: we waited: he went away.

This is a literary device that is probably better avoided by inexperienced punctuators.

Subtitles and subheadings

The colon is used between the title and subtitle of a book, film, etc:

Nearly five years ago, Helen Fielding published Bridget Jones: The Edge of Reason.
Leech, G N 1981 Semantics: The Study of Meaning

(For more on bibliographical references, see page 267.)

Similarly, colons may be used between two parts of a headline or chapter heading:

Modern art and the city: Webster attacks Glasgow's leaders
Disobedience: Man's Original Virtue

Capital letters or small letters following a colon?

When a colon introduces a list, the first word in the list should begin with a lower-case letter:

Inner-city communities all suffer from the same problems:
unemployment, poverty, poor health, squalor and misery.

To assess your claim, we need the following things:
  your fully filled-in claim form
  a copy of . . .

However, if the listed items are complete sentences, they should be punctuated as sentences, with capital letters at the beginning and full stops at the end:

The rules for visitors are as follows:
  1) You can only stay in the UK for 6 months.
  2) You will not be permitted to work whilst in the UK.
  3) You must not . . .

When a colon introduces an explanation, a summing-up, etc, what follows should begin with a lower-case letter:

There's something I have been meaning to tell you: it seems they're going to build a supermarket across the road.

American English often has a capital letter in this position:

Now a compromise has been struck: The casino will be 198 feet tall, not 300 feet.

For capital and small letters in quotations, see page 232.

American English
Unlike full stops and commas (see pages 46 and 126), colons are placed *outside* quotation marks:

They have struck a "compromise": the casino will only be 198 feet tall.

Other uses of the colon
• Ratios
Colons are used between numbers to indicate ratios:

26:39 = 2:3

• Clock times
In American English, a colon is used between the hours and the minutes when writing the time:

The movie starts at 6:15 pm.

British English normally uses a full stop (although the colon is coming more into use in British English also; see page 55):

The meeting closed at 5.05 pm.

• Book references
Chapter and verse references, for example to the Bible, are often separated by a colon:

Ephesians 3:10

• **Examples**

Colons are also often used to introduce examples, as in this book.

• **Memos**

Colons are used after headings in certain types of business correspondence, such as memos:

To: . . .
From: . . .
Date: . . .
Re: . . .

Summary of key points

- A colon is used to introduce a part of a sentence that explains, completes or elaborates on what has gone before.
- A colon is used to introduce a list. It may sometimes be followed by a dash.
- A colon may be used instead of a comma before direct speech and quotations.
- A colon may be used in sentences where one part is balanced against or contrasted with the other.

10
Dashes

The dash is seductive; it tempts the writer to use it as a punctuation-maid-of-all-work that saves him the trouble of choosing the right stop.

Sir Ernest Gowers, *Plain Words*

If this was true in Gowers's day (he was writing in the 1940s), it is probably no less true today. Of course, by this point in the book, *you* will already have given up any sloppy punctuation habits you once had. You will now be using full stops and commas and semicolons with confidence, so it is time to learn the *correct* uses of the dash.

Separating dashes and linking dashes

In printing, the two commonest dashes are the **m-dash** or **m-rule** and the **n-dash** or **n-rule**, so called because they correspond in length to the width of the letters *m* and *n* respectively. The n-dash is twice as long as a hyphen. (In handwriting, it is quite normal and correct to use only one length of dash, but it should always be noticeably longer than a hyphen.)

Dashes have two main functions. They may be **separating dashes**, used to separate off comments in much the same way as round brackets:

You can be a good socialist – as many people are, I believe – and still enjoy good food and good wines.

. . . or **linking dashes**, used to link words in much the same way as hyphens:

When the universe was created, so was the space–time continuum.

In the past, separating dashes were usually m-dashes and linking dashes n-dashes, but practice has now changed to some extent. It is quite normal in current British practice to use n-dashes for both purposes, as in the two examples above, though it is not incorrect still to use m-dashes as separators. (In America, separating dashes are generally m-dashes.)

Notice that n-dashes used as separating dashes are preceded and followed by a blank space whereas when they are used as linking dashes, there are no blank spaces. When m-dashes are used as separators, the blank spaces are optional and often omitted:

You can be a good socialist—as many people are, I believe— and still enjoy good food and good wines.

Hyphen or dash?

It is not uncommon to see hyphens used instead of dashes, both separating and linking. While this usually causes no confusion, there seems no real need or justification for it: there are various ways of producing dashes on a word-processor (which is what most people use nowadays) and therefore no good reason not to use them. If for some reason you cannot make a dash, a double hyphen is a good substitute.

The separating dash

Interruptions and comments
Separating dashes are used to separate off an interruption in a sentence:

The virus – highly contagious among chickens – is believed to spread to humans through contact with infected birds.
With hindsight – always the best view – his decision to resign was no real surprise.

Occasionally a non-defining relative clause (see page 102) may be separated off by dashes rather than the normal commas:

The men – who were both in their sixties – were immediately rushed to hospital.

Of course, if a comment comes at the end of a sentence, then only one dash is needed:

In January he opened a restaurant in Moscow – the first proper Chinese restaurant there.
I married beneath me – all women do.

Nancy Astor

She's the sort of woman who lives for others – you can always tell the others by their hunted expression.

C S Lewis

Commas, dashes or parentheses?

Both dashes and parentheses make stronger interruptions than commas. Dashes make stronger interruptions than parentheses:

The viewers I spoke to, all having expected a heated debate, said they had been very disappointed.

Channel 4 said an average of 8.3 million viewers (41% of the audience) watched the show.

The final show was watched by nine million viewers – 48% of the audience share – as the 27-year-old Surrey bank clerk fended off all challengers to win with nearly four million votes.

After half a mile the pain became (this is no exaggeration) absolute agony.

After half a mile the pain became – this is no exaggeration – absolute agony.

Dashes are also considered more informal than parentheses, and so should not be used in formal contexts.

It is recommended by some authorities that one should not use dashes round a comment consisting of more than one sentence because it might appear to the reader that the comment stopped at the end of the first sentence rather than continuing through to the second dash. It is a small point but one worth keeping in mind. If there could be confusion, use brackets instead.

Dashes for emphasis

A separating dash may be used to indicate a pause that emphasizes what follows:

The one thing you need is – patience.
He has been invited to everyone's house – once.
He can do it – and he will!

A separating dash may introduce a clause beginning with a conjunction, the dash again marking a pause that emphasizes what follows:

They didn't spend all their time together – and that's why their marriage worked so well.
If the number of journeys made on this bus service does not increase, the service will be discontinued – so use it or lose it!
This is the story of everyday life in a fishing community – although being set in the present time it is realistic about how much actual fishing goes on in such communities.
Authors are easy to get on with – if you're fond of children.

Michael Joseph (publisher)

With a punctuation mark such as a comma, or no punctuation mark at all, the break between the clauses is weaker and there is therefore less emphasis on what is said in the second part. Compare the following and notice how the emphasis increases and the nuances change as the break becomes stronger:

He says he's young at heart but slightly older in other places.
(almost purely factual)
He says he's young at heart, but slightly older in other places.
(with a little more emphasis on the contrast)
He says he's young at heart – but slightly older in other places.
(much more humorous)

A dash is often used to say to the reader, 'Wait for it, there's something interesting or unexpected coming':

Mrs Travers was surprised to hear her car engine purring – until she lifted the bonnet and discovered a cat.

A comma is correct for a statement of fact:

I couldn't see what was wrong with the engine, until I lifted the bonnet and discovered a cat sleeping there.

Narrative insertions

A pair of dashes may be used in a narrative to separate off something inserted into the middle of a description or passage of speech:

He had kept the boys waiting outside his study for nearly twenty minutes – 'Let them sweat a bit,' he'd remarked to the deputy head – and was intending to keep them there a while longer.
'Oh, please, constable' – she clasped her hands in supplication – 'let me in to see my son.'
'I didn't see my programme, because the television –' at this, he glared at me '– was tuned to the other side.'

Notice from the last two examples that the dashes can be inside or outside the quotation marks.

Incomplete sentences

A dash is used to indicate that a sentence has been cut off abruptly and is incomplete:

'Give me that back, or I'll –' 'Or you'll what? You and whose army?'

'My luggage has been –' 'Stolen?'
'It's all rather difficult to explain, but –' 'But you'll try to make up some sort of semi-convincing tale?'

If the interruption breaks a word, the dash should be attached directly to the unfinished word:

As I was just say–

Sometimes an m-dash is used here even when all the other dashes in a text are n-dashes:

As I was just say—

Note that since a dash marks a sentence that has come to an abrupt stop without being completed, it is not followed by a full stop. For the same reason, the dash is not followed by a comma in direct speech before a verb of speaking:

'Give me that back, or I'll –' he said.

However, an incomplete sentence may be followed by a question mark or an exclamation mark:

And you are – ?
What about you, Pet–? Oh, could somebody wake Peter up, please.
What the –!

A dash is also used to indicate a sentence that is broken off and followed by an unrelated sentence or clause:

It's just – well, it's not very nice.
I never cry. Even when my mother died, I – but enough of that, what about you?
I had hoped that someday – but it doesn't matter now.

Dash or ellipsis?

A dash marks a more abrupt end to a sentence than an ellipsis mark (...). An ellipsis mark should be used when a sentence does not stop abruptly but tails off as if there could be more to come:

You're still looking at me in that funny way ...

Marking a pause or hesitation

He wasn't a bad boy at heart, he was just young and free and – impulsive.
Of course I'm interested, it's a – a fascinating subject.
Well, I – er – I – um – I – I don't really know what to say.
One – two – three – go!

Lists

A dash can introduce a list:

This is what makes for a good story – the characters should be interesting, the action gripping or moving, and the ending unexpected but believable.

In formal writing, a colon should be used:

This is what makes for a good story: the characters should be interesting, the action gripping or moving, and the ending unexpected but believable.

Summing up and referring back

While a colon is used to introduce words that expand on or complete what has gone before, it is usually a dash that is used to introduce words that sum up or refer back to what has gone before:

There are three things we need: more time, more money and more help.
More time, more money and more help – these are the three things we need.

Sitting on a beach, listening to Bach, walking over hills – these are the things I like best of all.
Plates, cups, saucers, sugar bowl, milk jug – everything went flying.

A dash is used when a word or phrase is repeated:

We have laws in this country – laws that must be obeyed.
The Common Law of England has been laboriously built about a mythical figure – the figure of the 'Reasonable Man'.

A P Herbert

A spectre is haunting Europe – the spectre of Communism.

Karl Marx

Definitions

Like the colon, the dash may be used in definitions:

A classic – something that everybody wants to have read and nobody wants to read.

Mark Twain

Links

In informal writing, dashes are used to link clauses:

Do please come on the 29th – it should be an interesting evening.
I'm 26 years old – I really shouldn't have to be dealing with this kind of thing.

In more formal writing, other punctuation marks should be used as links: see the chapters on the comma, the colon and the semicolon. Sometimes there should be no link, and a full stop is more appropriate.

The linking dash

The linking dash functions as a linking element between words, in much the same way as a hyphen. The linking dash has two main uses, for which a hyphen is not appropriate.

Indicating ranges

The linking dash is used to indicate a range or extent between two points:

the 1914–1918 war
pages 54–67
volumes I–III
An A–Z Guide to the Whiskies of Scotland

Note that there is no space before or after the n-dash.

- Two common errors
- While a dash can be used to indicate a range, it must not be used in phrases with 'from' or 'between':

✗ *from 1914–1918*
✗ *between 1914–1918*

These are the correct forms:

✓ *from 1914 to 1918*
✓ *between 1914 and 1918*

- It is better not to use a dash to indicate a range when it would be juxtaposed with a hyphen:

✓ *a course for 16- to 18-year-olds*
✗ *a course for 16- –18-year-olds*

The following are definitely wrong:

✗ *16–18-year-olds* (hyphen missing after '16')
✗ *16–18 year-olds* (two hyphens missing after '16' and '18')
✗ *16- 18-year-olds* (three hyphens but no dash)

Linking two or more descriptive words

When two or more words together describe a following noun but do not form a compound word, they should be linked by linking dashes, not hyphens:

the space–time continuum
the Paris–Dakar race
the Catholic–Protestant divide
the Sapir–Whorf hypothesis (Sapir and Whorf are two people)
the Feynman–Gell-Mann hypothesis (by Feynman and Gell-Mann)

A hyphen is correct when the linked elements form a genuine compound:

the Franco-Prussian war
Indo-Chinese tigers
Anglo-American relations
(The *o* ending of the first parts of these words shows that they are compound-forming elements, not separate words.)
Alsace-Lorraine (considered as a single region)

The long dash

A dash longer than an m-dash is used to indicate the omission of letters, especially in swear-words or obscenities:

F—— you!
Get those f——g sheep off the road!

Asterisks are also used for this purpose:

Why do newspapers always write f*** instead of just spelling the word out?

Formerly a long dash was used when a writer did not want to spell out a name:

I was living in L—— at that time.
He was the cousin of Lord M——.

Summary of key points

- Dashes are used to separate off comments, explanations, etc that interrupt sentences or are added on at the ends of sentences.
- Dashes make stronger interruptions than parentheses.
- A dash is used at the end of a sentence that is broken off abruptly.
- A dash may introduce words that sum up or refer back to what has gone before.
- In informal writing, dashes can be used to link clauses.
- A dash is used to indicate a range or extent.
- A dash is used between two or more words that are closely linked but do not form a compound word.
- Dashes may be used to indicate the omission of letters.

11
Quotation marks

Joyce [the Irish writer James Joyce] favoured light punctuation and disliked quotation marks, calling them perverted commas.

The Oxford Companion to the English Language

Quotation marks, also known as 'quotes' or 'inverted commas', are used (a) to indicate direct speech, (b) to indicate a quotation, and (c) to highlight something in a text, for any of various reasons.

Like brackets, quotation marks must always be used in pairs, one preceding and the other following the word or words to be separated off.

Single and double quotation marks

There are two types of quotation mark: single ('...') and double ("...").

British English tends to prefer single quotation marks, but double quotation marks are acceptable and are the usual form of quotation marks in handwritten texts. Double quotes are arguably better than single quotes, because they cannot be confused with apostrophes:

'I'll be back,' said Arnie.
"I'll be back," said Arnie.

American usage prefers double quotation marks.

Direct speech

Quotation marks are put round words spoken in direct speech:

'You must help her,' he said.
'Do you need all that?' asked Agnes.
'You'll be fine,' he assured her.

There should be no quotation marks round indirect speech:

✗ He assured her 'she'd be fine'.
✓ He assured her she'd be fine.

• Punctuation marks
Punctuation marks that are part of the direct speech are written inside the quotation marks:

'Shoo,' he said weakly. (with a comma replacing a full stop; see page 44)
'Why not?' he asked.
'Look out!' she shouted.

When a sentence of direct speech is split by the speech verb, a comma must be added at the point of the split. The comma generally goes inside the quotation marks:

'You,' he said, 'must help her.'

However, some people argue that when a comma is not part of the original sentence of direct speech, it should go outside the quotation marks, and only be placed inside the closing quotation mark when it belongs to the original sentence. Compare the following examples:

'You', he said, 'must help her.' (The sentence of direct speech is *You must help her*, with no comma; so the comma indicating the split in the sentence goes outside the quotation marks.)
'You, John,' he said, 'must help her.' (The sentence of direct speech is *You, John, must help her*, with a comma after *John*; so the comma indicating the split in the sentence goes inside the quotation marks.)

While this is a perfectly logical rule, with much to recommend it, it is not the rule that most people currently apply. It is more in keeping with current practice always to put the comma inside the closing quotation mark at a sentence split.

Note that there is also a comma after the verb of speaking when it splits a sentence:

'You,' he said, 'must help her.'

Omission of quotation marks

Quotation marks are not always necessary round direct speech, for example when what is being quoted is not part of a conversation but a person's thoughts or a rhetorical question:

Why me? he asked himself. Why always me?
You may ask, what is our aim? I'll tell you what our aim is. Victory.

And if the words are not the *exact* words that a person said or thought, there cannot be quotation marks:

Where were they going? he wondered. (His actual words, spoken or thought, would be 'Where *are* they going?')

Repetition of quotation marks
If a passage of direct speech goes beyond a single paragraph, each new paragraph should start with an opening quotation mark, but only the final paragraph should have a closing quotation mark.

Quotations
Short quotations integrated into a sentence should be marked off by quotation marks:

As Drummond says, 'the details of this population movement are unknown to us, because the records of the kingdom at that time have not yet been found'.
Dickens complained that he found Mrs Gaskell's North and South 'too wordy' and 'wearisome in the last degree'.
Many parents admit to feeling 'redundant' or 'empty' when their children have all left home.

Longer quotations should begin on a new line and should not be in quotation marks. They are usually preceded and followed by a blank line:

As Drummond says in The Hurrians:

The details of this population movement are unknown to us, because the records of the country at that time have not yet been found. But in the following century, the influence of Hurrian culture is very marked.

For more about quotation styles, see page 269.

Quoting exact words

Only the *exact* words that a person said or wrote should be inside the quotation marks:

✗ *Speaking on behalf of the Government, the Prime Minister said 'that they would be tough on crime and tough on the causes of crime'.*

Wrong! What were the Prime Minister's actual words? 'We will be tough on crime and tough on the causes of crime.' He did not actually *say* the words 'that they would be tough on crime and tough on the causes of crime', so these words cannot be given as the quotation.

There are two ways of quoting the Prime Minister correctly. Firstly, you could move the opening quotation mark to a point in the sentence where it *does* mark the beginning of words said by the Prime Minister:

✓ *Speaking on behalf of the Government, the Prime Minister said that they would be 'tough on crime and tough on the causes of crime'.*

Alternatively, you could quote the exact words spoken:

✓ *Speaking on behalf of the Government, the Prime Minister said: 'We will be tough on crime and tough on the causes of crime.'*

Quotations within quotations

If a second set of quotation marks is needed within the first set, you should use double quotes within single quotes and single quotes within double quotes:

'What does "kleptomania" mean?' he asked.
"What does 'octane' mean?" she asked.
"The worst thing for us would be for the audience to say, 'Well, I suppose they were all right,'" he said.
'I don't like it when people go around saying "I'm English." Who cares?'

If you need to have quotes within quotes, then it's single–double–single or double–single–double.

Highlighting

Quotation marks are used to highlight something in a passage of writing for any of various reasons. It may be to pick out a word that is being referred to; a translation of a foreign word; a technical or slang word or an invented expression; a reference to a well-known saying, proverb, story, etc; or a punning or joking use of a word; as in the following examples:

The word 'dodo' comes from Portuguese doudo, *meaning 'fool'.*
There are two t's in 'bottle'.
His name is Anmol, which is Hindi for 'priceless'.
He called them a bunch of chavs. What on earth are 'chavs'?
Bournemouth is one of the few English towns that one can safely call 'her'.

John Betjeman

The question 'What now?' is one that no-one in the Middle East can answer confidently.

He said it was 'really groovy' to be there. Do people really still talk like that?
In this book, I am adopting a 'stratificational' approach to grammar, though not that of Lamb and Lockwood.
I'm calling it a 'thingometer'.
Perhaps the name for a book of puns should be a 'punnet'!

Quotation marks are used to pick out words for emphasis:

It's not a question of 'entertaining' readers or setting out to 'change lives'.
The distinction in those days was between the man who was 'a gentleman' and the man who was 'not a gentleman'.
Some old folk don't claim their means-tested benefits because they know that any savings they possess are the 'means' that have to be disclosed for testing.

Quotation marks are used when you are quoting someone else's words:

The builders offered a 'complete service' but all they did was make a complete mess.

Quotation marks may be used when you are critical of what someone else has said or of the way they have used a word, and you want to draw attention to it or distance yourself from it. Quotation marks also indicate irony:

Robert's father was a Hutu, his mother was a Tutsi, and that was the 'reason' he murdered her. (The writer does not accept this as a valid reason.)
Here 'by chance' we met other 'prisoners'. (The writer does not believe it was a chance meeting, nor that the people they

met were actually prisoners – it was a planned meeting and they were spies.)

In the 1980s and early 1990s many companies felt entitled to take 'holidays' from their pension fund contributions.

Pensions were often 'mis-sold' (often a euphemism for fraud) on a grand scale.

Quotation marks are used to pick out something that does not fit grammatically into the sentence as a whole:

The Scottish parliament building is very 'look at me' and 'look at this'.

Notice the use of the quotation marks and hyphens in the following examples:

a 'can do' attitude
a can-do attitude
The man nodded a 'good morning' as I drew level.
The man nodded a good-morning as I drew level.

Quotation marks are used with nicknames:

I learned to play the guitar from a book by Bert 'Mr Guitar' Weedon.

He was an associate of the famous Chicago gangster Al 'Scarface' Capone.

Do not overdo highlighting. You should only use highlighting quotation marks if they actually serve a purpose.

Book titles, etc

Quotation marks may be put round the title of a book, film, play, television programme, magazine, etc, or the name of a ship, theatre, restaurant, etc:

✓ *We're staying at 'The Red Lion'.*
✓ *We're staying at the Red Lion.*

The pamphlet was headed 'To the Sons of the Motherland!'
Isn't there a speech in 'Macbeth' that starts something like 'Tomorrow and tomorrow and tomorrow'?
I never watch 'The Simpsons'.
Nearly five years ago, Helen Fielding published 'Bridget Jones: The Edge of Reason', a sequel to the enormously successful 'Bridget Jones's Diary'.
The ship was called the 'Mary Rose'.

However, this is often not done nowadays if it is not necessary for clarity.

Titles of books and plays can also be underlined in writing or be in italics in printing.

Notice that when 'the' is part of the title it goes inside the quotation marks but when it is not part of the title it goes outside the quotation marks:

I never watch 'The Simpsons'.
The ship was called the 'Mary Rose'.

For quotation marks round the titles of articles in journals or chapters of books, see page 268.

Punctuation in direct speech and quoted matter

The correct choice and placement of punctuation marks around quotation marks causes many problems, especially when there are quotation marks next to other quotation marks at the end of a sentence. However, if the problems are approached in a logical, step-by-step fashion, a pattern can be seen that is not hard to understand or put into practice. There is not total agreement among authorities on how to handle punctuation around quotation marks, but the following can be regarded as a reasonable and logical statement of the principles.

In this section 'quoted words' means 'anything within quotation marks', be it an actual quotation, a passage of direct speech or anything else that is highlighted by means of quotation marks.

A quotation that is not a sentence

When a sentence ends with quoted words that are not a complete sentence, the sentence ends with only one punctuation mark, placed outside the closing quotation mark:

He called me a 'chav'.
What's a 'chav'?
Don't you dare call me a 'chav'!

A quotation that is a complete sentence

When the end of quoted words that are a complete sentence coincides with the end of the sentence they are included in, you would expect there to be two punctuation marks, one *inside* the quotation mark to indicate the end of the quoted words and one *outside* to indicate the end of the whole sentence; for example:

Before he hit the ball, he shouted 'Fore!'.

However, in practice, when the punctuation mark *outside* the quotation mark would be a full stop, it is omitted:

I heard someone behind me in the queue say, 'My feet hurt.'
The lieutenant leapt to his feet, shouting: 'Charge!'
I said to him, 'I beg your pardon?'

The rules are different for quoted words that are fully integrated into the sentence. For them, the full stop goes *outside* the quotation mark. Compare these examples:

As Shakespeare once said, 'All the world's a stage.' (quotation a separate unit, separated off by the comma; full stop at end of quotation)
Shakespeare once said that 'all the world's a stage'. (quotation fully part of the larger sentence because of the linking word 'that'; full stop at end of whole sentence)

When the final punctuation mark is a question mark or an exclamation mark, the rules are a little more complicated.
1. When the punctuation mark at the end of the quoted words is a full stop, omit it:

✗ *Why did you say, 'You're a prat.'?*
✓ *Why did you say, 'You're a prat'?*

2. When there is a question mark followed by an exclamation mark, or vice versa, both are kept:

Did you remember to shout 'Fore!'?
She screamed at him: 'Why should we?'!

When both punctuation marks would be the same, it is correct to put both in; for example, with question marks:

Why did she say, 'Who are you?'?

. . . but much more commonly one or other of them is dropped:

Why did she say, 'Who are you?'
Why did she say, 'Who are you'?

If you do drop one question mark, it must not be one that is the sole indication that a sentence is a question:

Who was it who said, 'George Bush has won again?' ('George Bush has won again' is a question.)
Who was it who said, 'George Bush has won again'? ('George Bush has won again' is a statement.)

Quotations within quotations
The problems really start when there are quotation marks inside quotation marks at the end of a sentence. Notice the different position of the full stop at the end of these examples:

Tom said, 'Tim called me a "prat".'
Tom said, 'According to Shakespeare, "All the world's a stage."'

However, the problem is much less formidable than many people think. All you need to do is approach it on the basis of the principles given above.
1. In the first example, *prat* is not a sentence, so there

is no full stop after it. *Tim called me a "prat"* is a sentence, so it ends with a full stop. Compare:

He called me a 'chav'.
Tim called me a "prat".

Tom said, 'Tim called me a "chav".' is also a sentence and could theoretically end with a full stop, but as we have already seen, when there is a full stop before a closing quotation mark, you drop the full stop after it:

I heard someone behind me in the queue say, 'My feet hurt.'
Tom said, 'Tim called me a "chav".'

2. If the 'innermost' quoted words are a sentence, then they end with a full stop. *All the world's a stage* is a sentence, so it ends with a full stop:

"All the world's a stage."

According to Shakespeare, "All the world's a stage." is also a sentence, but as we have seen, when there is a full stop before a closing quotation mark, you drop the full stop after it:

According to Shakespeare, "All the world's a stage."

Tom said, 'According to Shakespeare "All the world's a stage."' is also a sentence, but again there is no full stop at the end of it because there is already a full stop after *stage*:

Tom said, 'According to Shakespeare, "All the world's a stage."'

So very easily, by the rules that were established for relatively simple sentences, it is possible to establish the punctuation pattern for more complex sentences.

You start with the innermost quoted words, and decide what punctuation mark, if any, is required at the end of them:

Tom said, 'xxxxxx "xxxxx ↓ "'

Then you move one place to the right and decide what punctuation mark, if any, you should put there:

Tom said, 'xxxxxx "xxxxx" ↓'

Then you move right again and decide what punctuation mark, if any, you should put there:

Tom said, 'xxxxxx "xxxxx"' ↓

No matter how complicated your sentence is, by working systematically from left to right and applying the rules used in punctuating simpler sentences, you can always decide on the correct punctuation marks.

Sometimes, however, you may have to go back and change your decision. Consider this sentence:

Tom said, 'Why did you say, "You're a prat"?'

By applying the left-to-right principle, you will start off by putting a full stop after *You're a prat* because it's a sentence:

"You're a prat."

But when you come to '*Why did you say, "You're a prat."?*', you will realize that, because there is a question mark at the end of that sentence, there shouldn't be a full stop at the end of the included sentence (see page 178):

✗ *Why did you say, "You're a prat."?*
✓ *Why did you say, "You're a prat"?*

Moving right again, you know that when there is a question mark at the end of quoted words, there is no full stop after the quotation mark (see page 65); so the whole sentence will be correctly punctuated with one question mark and no full stops:

Tom said, 'Why did you say, "You're a prat"?'

British and American practice
The above rules apply to British English. American English differs in some respects. If the quotation is not a complete sentence, the full stop goes *outside* the quotation marks in British English but *inside* the quotation marks in American English:

The police have warned that it is not a question of 'whether' a terrorist attack will occur, but 'when'.
We cater for everyone 'from the cradle to the grave'.

It seems that the issue is no longer "if" this will happen but "how soon."
The artificial trees are available in heights from "6 to 40 feet."

The same is true for commas: outside in British English but inside in American English:

The song, which is called 'From Here to There', is a beautiful ballad.
This is the greatest threat I can think of to the "American ideal," whatever that means.

Summary of key points

- Quotation marks are used to indicate direct speech, to indicate a quotation, and to highlight some element of a sentence.
- Quotation marks can be placed round book titles, etc.
- Great care must be taken to place punctuation correctly and to omit punctuation marks that are not required.

12
Brackets

*('You listen to this,' said my sister to me, in a severe
parenthesis.)*

Charles Dickens, *Great Expectations*

There are four types of brackets: **round brackets** or
parentheses ( ), **square brackets** [ ], **curly brackets** or
braces { }, and **angle brackets** < >. Of these four, the
last two have specialized uses in mathematics, science
and linguistics that are beyond the scope of a general
book on punctuation such as this.

Remember that brackets always come in pairs, one
before and one after the bracketed words.

Round brackets

Interruptions and comments
Round brackets are mainly used to separate off comments and other interruptions or add-ons (see page 93):

*It was agreed that the milk and the windfall apples (and also
the main crop of apples when they ripened) should be reserved
for the pigs alone.*

George Orwell, *Animal Farm*

It wasn't that she didn't find him attractive (or was it that, perhaps?).
'What on earth are you doing in there?' (Her tone was a mixture of slight concern and rising suspicion.)

Take care with other punctuation marks, placing them in the correct position inside or outside the brackets. When words in parentheses form a complete and independent sentence, the punctuation mark they end with should be *inside* the closing bracket:

He also drew the illustrations for the book. (That was something he very rarely did.)
I didn't tell her what had happened. (How could I have?) I just said I'd been asleep.

When words in brackets are included within a larger sentence, the punctuation mark should be *outside* the closing bracket:

The bath and washbasin had gold-plated taps (the sort I always associate with 'conspicuous consumption').
Be prepared for other people to disagree with your decision (perhaps quite strongly), but don't let them persuade you that you are wrong.

However, an included comment may sometimes need punctuation of its own, in which case the punctuation goes *inside* the brackets:

Chapter by chapter, the correct uses (and also many of the wrong uses!) of each of the punctuation marks is explained.

When the included comment is a statement, there is no full stop after it inside the brackets:

Eventually I ended up outside Wharfdale Shopping Centre (the place I had visited the day before), and looked for somewhere to eat.

Brackets, commas or dashes?

Brackets make stronger breaks in sentences than commas:

He stood on the lawn, a blanket round his shoulders, and watched his house go up in flames.
He stood on the lawn (he had a blanket round his shoulders) and watched his house go up in flames.

If the comment is a sentence in its own right, as in the second example, it cannot go between commas: it must be cordoned off by punctuation that makes a stronger break. It is even possible for there to be more than one sentence enclosed in brackets, in which case the punctuation is as in the following example:

He stood on the lawn (he had a blanket round his shoulders. It was the colour of the setting sun) and watched his house go up in flames.

Dashes are considered more informal than brackets, and so should not be used in formal contexts:

✓ *Application forms (three copies) should be sent to the Person-nel Manager.*

✗ *Application forms – three copies – should be sent to the Personnel Manager.*

Dashes also make stronger breaks than brackets and can be used for your own comments:

The letter said, 'Application forms (twelve copies)' – twelve copies! – 'should be sent to the Personnel Manager.'

Alternatives

Brackets may be used to show alternative forms:

The name(s) and address(es) of your sponsor(s) should be included with your application.

Additional information

Additional information of various kinds is often enclosed in round brackets:

The Plant Sciences Research Programme (PSP) is one of 10 research programmes funded by the Rural Livelihoods Department for the Department for International Development (DFID).
TNT (trinitrotoluene) was developed around the time of the Second World War.
John Donne (1572–1631) was a leading English poet of the Metaphysical school.
The next meeting of the Association will be on the first Tuesday of next month (December 7).

Letters and numbers in lists

Parentheses may be used round letters and numbers in lists; for example:

The matters to be discussed are:
> *(a) print run*
> *(b) price*
> *(c) jacket*
> *(d) publication date*
> *(e) marketing strategy*

The rules for visitors are as follows:
  1) *You can only stay in the UK for 6 months.*
  2) *You will not be permitted to work whilst in the UK.*
  3) *You must not intend to study.*
  4) *You must have adequate accommodation.*
  5) *You must have the finances to support yourself for the duration of your stay.*
  6) *You must be able to meet the cost of your onward journey.*

The second example gives an instance of when, contrary to the general rule, it is correct to have a single bracket rather than a pair.

Square brackets

Square brackets are used to enclose letters, words or phrases that are not in the original text but which have been added by someone as comments, corrections, explanations, etc:

In that time, no one in Italy, not even Giovanni Agnelli [the head of Fiat], drove round in a limousine.

Michael Palin, *Hemingway Adventure*

(What the original speaker actually said was 'In that time, no one in Italy, not even Giovanni Agnelli, drove round in a limousine.' The information in square brackets has been added by Michael Palin for the benefit of the reader who, it is assumed, would not know who Giovanni Agnelli was.)

They [the forebears of the Janjaweed] immigrated 12 centuries ago from the deserts of the Arabian Peninsula.

She [Bridget] is neurotic, smug, conscious of every ounce of cellulite.

An alternative style that can be used where appropriate is to replace the part that needs to be explained with the explanation in square brackets:

[The forebears of the Janjaweed] immigrated 12 centuries ago from the deserts of the Arabian Peninsula.
[Bridget] is neurotic, smug, conscious of every ounce of cellulite.

Square brackets are also used to enclose editorial comments:

According to this book, Endison [sic] began working on the light bulb in 1878. ('[sic]' shows that the writer knows that the name should be 'Edison', not 'Endison', but is quoting the text exactly as it was originally written; it means 'I know this is a mistake; it isn't my mistake.')
Tony Blair said he was going to be tough on crime and tough *on the causes of crime [my emphasis].* (Here the person quoting the Prime Minister is emphasizing one particular point in the quotation and is drawing attention to the fact that they are doing so.)

On the other hand, if the *original* writer wants to comment on something in what they are writing, *round* brackets should be used.

Brackets within brackets
When it is necessary to have brackets within brackets, it may be confusing (though it is not wrong) to have one pair of round brackets within another pair. In that case, it is correct to use square brackets inside round brackets or vice versa:

The deceased (John Smith [aka John Smithson]) resided at 14 Chestnut Grove.

Summary of key points

- Round brackets are used to separate off comments, additional information, etc.
- Round brackets make a greater break in a sentence than commas but a weaker break than dashes.
- Dashes are more informal than round brackets.
- Square brackets are used for editorial comments and corrections.

13
Ellipsis

The ellipsis is my favorite writing tool, because you can save so much work by just letting the reader figure it out.

Andy Saunders

Ellipsis is represented by three full stops, sometimes separated by thin spaces (. . .) but nowadays often not (...). Ellipsis points are used to indicate where something has been omitted from a quotation, to punctuate sentences that tail off leaving something unsaid or implied, to indicate pauses, and to form links between parts of sentences.

Ellipsis marks indicating omissions

Omissions in quotations

Ellipsis dots are used in quoted material to show that the quotation does not include the complete text of the original but that some word or words have been omitted. The ellipsis can be at the beginning, in the middle or at the end of a text. For example, consider this sentence from *The Grammar, History and Derivation of the English Language* by Evan Daniel:

All the facts with which a grammar deals are to be found in the language to which the grammar belongs; and it is in the language itself, not in books, that these facts are primarily to be sought.

This sentence could, when being quoted, be shortened in various ways by the omission of parts that are not needed for the purposes of the person quoting it. The omission would be marked by ellipses:

As Evan Daniel says in The Grammar, History and Derivation of the English Language, *'. . . it is in the language itself, not in books, that these facts are primarily to be sought.'*

As Evan Daniel says in The Grammar, History and Derivation of the English Language, *'All the facts with which a grammar deals are to be found in the language to which the grammar belongs; and it is in the language itself . . . that these facts are primarily to be sought.'*

As Evan Daniel says in The Grammar, History and Derivation of the English Language, *'All the facts with which a grammar deals are to be found in the language to which the grammar belongs; . . .'*

An ellipsis may be placed in square brackets, but this is not common.

The omission marked by an ellipsis may be a matter of delicacy:

Get the . . . out of my way!

Uncompleted sentences

Ellipsis marks are used to show uncompleted sentences or sentences that, although grammatically complete, imply that something has been left unsaid:

Honestly, Jo, you're impossible . . .

Perhaps one day I will understand his motives; perhaps one day he will explain them to me; perhaps we will even . . . Oh, but this is just being silly, isn't it?

I can just imagine him going home in a terrible temper and dashing off a letter to the manager: 'Dear Sir, I wish to complain in the strongest possible terms . . .'

The press were just beginning to forget about us, and now . . .

I don't think that was a very good idea . . .

'Ah, yes. You're Jones. And your job is to . . . ?' 'Well, I, er, I, um, . . .'

The first part of our marriage was very happy. But then, on the way back from the ceremony . . .

Henny Youngman

Dash or ellipsis points?

Ellipsis marks a sentence that tails off. For an uncompleted sentence that breaks off abruptly, use a dash:

'Look here, I had just –'

Punctuation with ellipsis

When an ellipsis indicates an uncompleted sentence, it should not be followed by a full stop. According to some authorities, if the ellipsis comes at the end of a sentence that is grammatically complete (the ellipsis merely leaving something implied), you should add a full stop as well, but this is a subtlety that is generally ignored. Three dots are enough.

An ellipsis can, of course, be followed by a question mark or an exclamation mark:

Ah, yes. You're Jones. And your job is to . . . ?

Any punctuation mark that occurs before an ellipsis, whether within or at the end of a sentence, should be retained:

There is no science that is not capable of additions; . . . If this be true of all other sciences, why not of morals? . . . The very conception of this as possible is in the highest degree encouraging.

William Godwin, *Enquiry Concerning Political Justice*

Ellipsis marks indicating hesitation or pause

An ellipsis may indicate a slight pause or hesitation:

Until that morning, his life had been . . . well, dull, really.
Their Royal Family are like . . . living saints.
It wouldn't be wise to tell them, would it? About you and me . . . and what we did?
Lara? . . . It's Ken.

A dash marks a shorter or more abrupt pause:

Of course I'm interested, it's a – a fascinating subject.

The pause may be for dramatic or comic effect:

He opened the box and found . . . nothing!
You've got to laugh, haven't you? Now, take my wife . . . please.

In informal writing and journalism, an ellipsis is often used to form a loose link between clauses and sentences:

We were all thinking . . . was every one of the remaining 59 days going to be equally hard?
Tired of aerobics? Tired of fad diets? To really lose weight . . . try pole dancing.

In such cases, there is usually an element of pausing for effect. If there is no sense of pausing for effect, use other punctuation marks. Do not use the pause ellipsis at all in formal writing.

Ellipsis marks as links within sentences

Ellipsis points may be used to indicate a link between two or more parts of a sentence that are interrupted by something else, as is done occasionally in this book. See for example page 100.

Summary of key points

- Ellipsis is used to indicate where something has been omitted from a quotation, to punctuate sentences that leave something unsaid or implied, and to indicate pauses.
- Ellipsis points may also be used to link parts of sentences that are separated by other material.

14
Obliques

The oblique is also called the **solidus** or the **slash** (especially in email addresses).

In computing, it is sometimes necessary to distinguish between a forward slash (/) and a backslash (\).

Alternatives
The oblique is used to indicate alternatives:

Dear Sir/Madam, . . .
Whatever he/she does and whatever happens to him/her affects others as well.
Symptoms will include dizziness and difficulty with vision and/or balance.
Temperatures can rise above 50°C/122°F in high summer.

Linking items
The oblique is used to indicate places on a route, etc:

The 11.55 London/Manchester train has been cancelled.
The patient suffered the first spasms on the New York/Amsterdam flight.

This can also be done by means of a short dash:

the Paris–Dakar rally

Other words can be linked in a similar way:

Glasgow-born singer/songwriter Ken Burns
Painter/decorator. No job too small

This can also be done with hyphens:

singer-songwriter   *player-manager*

Periods of time

Obliques are used to indicate periods of time:

the 2004/05 shinty season
the 2003/2004 financial year

Dates

Obliques can be used in writing dates:

9/11   *14/11/04*

Dates can also be written with dots instead of obliques:

14.11.2004

Quantities

In measurements, obliques can be used to express ratios:

The density of Neptune is 1.64 g/cm^3.

Abbreviations

Obliques can be used in certain abbreviations:

c/o (= 'care of')   *i/c* (= 'in charge of')   *a/c* (= 'account')

Fractions

Obliques can be used in writing fractions:

An obol was worth 1/6 of a drachma. The chalkos was worth 1/8 of an obol.

Poetry

If you quote poetry, you can write the lines out in two ways. One way is to write them as they were written, on separate lines:

Of all the trees in England,
From sea to sea again,
The Willow loveliest stoops her boughs
Beneath the driving rain.

Walter de la Mare, 'Trees'

The other way is to write them in continuous text, with obliques marking each new line:

As de la Mare says, 'Of all the trees in England, / From sea to sea again, / The Willow loveliest stoops her boughs / Beneath the driving rain.'

Internet website addresses

Obliques (in this case, usually called slashes or forward slashes) are used in writing website addresses:

www.bbc.co.uk/radio2

15
Apostrophes

Nearly all the leaflets were depressingly illiterate,
particularly with regard to punctuation – I sometimes
think that if I see one more tourist leaflet that says
'Englands Best' or 'Britains Largest' I will go and torch
the place.

Bill Bryson, *Notes from a Small Island*

As Bryson noticed on his tour round the United Kingdom, there are many, many people who do not understand the apostrophe. Things have become so bad that there is now even an Apostrophe Protection Society. Strangely, at the same time as the apostrophe is being lost as the marker of possession (*Englands Best, Britains Largest*), it is being increasingly used as a marker of plural nouns (*apple's and banana's*). Both are equally wrong.

The possessive apostrophe

One of the main uses of the apostrophe is to mark possessive forms:

John's books   *the boys' bikes*

The basic rule

The rule in its basic form is perfectly straightforward and comes in two parts:

1. The possessive form of a noun or name is made by adding *'s* to it:

   the boy's dog (= 'the dog belonging to the boy')
   the children's bikes (= 'the bikes belonging to the children')
   James's wife (= 'the wife of James')
   Robert Burns's poetry (= the poetry of Robert Burns')
   my brothers-in-law's cars (= 'the cars belonging to my brothers-in-law')
   the Laird of Cockpen's wig (= 'the wig belonging to the Laird of Cockpen')

2. But if the noun or name is plural and it already ends in *s*, add an apostrophe alone:

   the boys' dog (= 'the dog belonging to the boys')
   in two months' time (= 'after two months')

- With singular names ending in *s*, usage is variable:

Moses' army or *Moses's army*

The simple rule here is: write what you say. If you say /mohziziz/, write *Moses's*, but if you say /mohziz/, write *Moses'*. Similarly, depending on how you pronounce the words, you can correctly write *Burns's poetry* or *Burns' poetry* (but always *Burns Night* without an apostrophe).

The same applies to singular nouns ending in *s*, such as *species*:

DNA evidence indicates the species' fortunes went downhill 23,000 years before humans even made their mark in North America.

Again the rule is: write it as you say it.

Some compound nouns, originally formed with a possessive, are no longer written with an apostrophe:

Achilles' heel but *Achilles tendon*

But in some cases you just have to follow what others do: *St Thomas' Hospital* should be *Thomas's* (because that's how you say it) but it isn't.
Errors to watch for:

✗ *Les' email*
✗ *Gus' personal feelings*
✗ *He refused the waitress' offer of coffee.*
(The possessive forms should be *Les's, Gus's* and *waitress's* because that is how these words would be said.)
✗ *childrens clothes*
✗ *ladies shoe repair*
(These need apostrophes: *children's, ladies'.*)
✗ *childrens' clothes*
✗ *mens' shoe repair*
(The apostrophes are in the wrong place: *children's, men's.*)

Note, however, that no apostrophe is needed in a compound noun written as a single word:

menswear

Apostrophes have to be added to each noun individually:

✗ *donations of unwanted ladies, gents and children's clothing*
✓ *donations of unwanted ladies', gents' and children's clothing*

Possessive pronouns do not have apostrophes:

hers, ours, yours, theirs, its, whose

Note in particular the difference between *its* (= 'of it') and *it's* (= 'it is' or 'it has'), and *whose* (= 'of whom') and *who's* (= 'who is' or 'who has').

In expressions with *sake*, there may or may not be an apostrophe:

for heaven's sake but *for goodness sake*

Plural nouns

The basic rule
Plural nouns *do not* need an apostrophe. The following are all incorrect (and are examples of what is often called the 'greengrocer's apostrophe', though it seems unfair to pick on greengrocers as being especially guilty of this error):

✗ *pasta's and kebab's*
✗ *tomato's and lettuce's*
✗ *Property's for Sale or Rent*
✗ *CCTV camera's are in operation.*
✗ *Hairdresser requires model's for trainee's*

These are correct:

✓ *pastas and kebabs*
✓ *tomatoes and lettuces*
✓ *Properties for Sale or Rent*

✓ *CCTV cameras are in operation*
✓ *Hairdresser requires models for trainees*

Similarly, there are no apostrophes in plural names:

I'm tired of keeping up with the Joneses, and the Smiths, and the Browns.
There were two Lewises in my class in primary school.

However, allow a plural like *Louis's* where a regular form (*Louises*) could cause uncertainty: is it boys called 'Louis' or girls called 'Louise'?

Short words
The plurals of certain short words are often written with apostrophes:

She gave me a list of do's and don'ts. (Note the position of the apostrophe in don'ts.)
I feel there are really two me's at the moment.
Are the puppies he's or she's?
We have had several set-to's with them over this.

Forms without apostrophes are equally correct.

Quoted words
If a plural word is being quoted in a sentence, it is often written with an apostrophe, though the apostrophe can be omitted if there would be no confusion:

There are too many if's, but's, maybe's and possibly's in this proposal.

Similarly, if a plural noun is the title of a book, play, etc quoted in a sentence, it is better written with an apostrophe, though again it is correct to omit the apostrophe:

I've already seen three Hamlet's this year. (= three versions of Hamlet)

This can also be a change of typeface:

I've already seen three Hamlet's *this year.*

Letters

Plurals of lower-case letters or of abbreviations written wholly or partly in lower-case letters take apostrophes for clarity:

All that remains to do is dot some i's and cross some t's.
There were some very close appeals for lbw's.
She's got two PhD's, or are they MPhil's?

Plurals of capital letters or of abbreviations, etc written in capital letters do not require apostrophes, except for clarity:

MPs, TVs, WCs, ASBOs, GCSEs
What we need is a couple of JCBs.
Write a row of I's. (not . . . *row of Is*)

But apostrophes are needed for abbreviations with full stops:

M.P.'s, Ph.D.'s, W.C.'s.

The same is true for past tenses of abbreviations. An apostrophe may be needed for clarity:

The car needs to be M.O.T.'d or MOT'd.

Numbers

The plurals of single numbers are written with apostrophes:

Take away the 2's, then the 3's.

The plurals of longer numbers, dates, etc are better written without apostrophes, but it is not wrong to have one:

They lined up in 20s and 30s
the 1970s or the 1970's
They all drive 4x4s.

Omissions

Letters that have been omitted are usually indicated by apostrophes:

are not > *aren't*	*he will* > *he'll*
cannot > *can't*	*will not* > *won't*
have not > *haven't*	*do not* > *don't* (watch *do's and don'ts*)

Apostrophes are often used in this way in representations of informal speech and dialect:

She'd've done the same thing.
So'm I.
D'you like it?
I should never've trusted you!
That'd've made my day.
I know I shouldn't've said it.

Gi'e it tae me.
She went to sleep wi' a wee poke o' sweeties in her hand.

When *and* is shortened to *n*, there should be *two* apostrophes:

cheese 'n' onion crisps
rock 'n' roll

Some shortened forms of words and phrases are written with apostrophes even though the non-contracted forms are no longer in use; for example:

o'clock (from *of the clock*)
ne'er-do-well (from *never-do-well*)
Hallowe'en (from *All Hallow Even*; *Halloween* is also correct)
cat-o'-nine-tails
will-o'-the-wisp

Some contractions are out of date but still seen in poetry, etc:

e'en, o'er, 'tis and *'twas*

Many words that are in origin shortened forms are now words in their own right. They are not written with apostrophes:

bra, bus, cello, decaff, exam, flu, fridge, gym, phone, plane, pram, etc

Apostrophes indicating the omission of letters may sometimes be found in place-names:

Bo'ness (in West Lothian = 'Borrowstounness')
Jo'burg (= Johannesburg)

Apostrophes may also be used to indicate the omission of numbers, e.g. in dates:

during the '70s and '80s (in this case, do not put an apostrophe before the *s:* ✗ *the '70's*)
That happened back in '97, I think.

Apostrophes in foreign languages

Certain languages, such as Arabic and Chinese, require apostrophes when transliterated into English:

the Noble Qur'an
t'ai chi ch'uan

Make sure you put the apostrophes in and get them in the right place. If in doubt, check in your dictionary.

(There are actually two ways of transliterating Chinese into English: one requires apostrophes and the other does not. Hence one sees both *ch'i* and *qi*, *t'ai chi ch'uan* and *tai ji quan* or *taijiquan*.)

Plurals of foreign words may be written with apostrophes for clarity:

The title of the film Qian Li Zou Dan Ji *means 'Lone Ride over a Thousand Li's' (1* li *equals 0.31 mile).*

Keyboarding apostrophes

Take care when keyboarding words or numbers with initial apostrophes. You may have to correct ones that face the wrong way:

not '*tis* but '*tis*
not *rock* '*n*' *roll* but *rock* '*n*' *roll*
not '*70s* but '*70s*

Summary of key points

- Possessives are formed by adding '*s* to a noun or name, unless the noun or name is plural and ends in *s*, in which case only an apostrophe is added.
- Possessive forms of pronouns do not have apostrophes.
- Plurals are not usually written with apostrophes.
- Apostrophes are used to indicate where letters have been omitted.

16
Hyphens

If you take hyphens seriously, you will surely go mad.

John Benbow, *Manuscript and Proof*

Hyphens are used much less frequently now than they were formerly. Compound nouns, for example, that were formerly hyphenated (e.g. *tea-bag*) are now generally written either as two words (*tea bag*) or as single words (*teabag*). In the realm of punctuation, what were formerly *full-stops* are now *full stops* and *semi-colons* have become *semicolons*.

Sir Winston Churchill is reputed to have called hyphens 'a blemish to be avoided wherever possible', and in the opinion of the Fowlers in *The King's English*, hyphens are 'regrettable necessities . . . to be done away with when they reasonably may'.

However, correctly used, hyphens add clarity to writing by showing in black and white what stress and intonation would indicate in speech. Hyphens may be done away with 'when they reasonably may', but they cannot be done away with altogether. Compare the following examples and notice the difference the hyphens make:

little-known paths through the mountains (= 'not well known')
little known paths through the mountains (= 'small paths')

secret-weapon technology (= 'secret weapons')
secret weapon technology (= 'secret technology')

And if you think hyphens are unimportant, consider this question from American comedian George Carlin:

Which is taller, a short order cook or a small engine mechanic?

Descriptive phrases preceding nouns

The basic rule

When two or more words together form a phrase describing a following noun, they must be hyphenated:

A village on the east coast is an east-coast *village.*
The people who live next door are your next-door *neighbours.*
Instructions that are easy to follow are easy-to-follow *instructions.*

Note that such phrases only require hyphens when they *precede* the noun they describe, but not elsewhere:

✓ *An* easy-to-use *adhesive is easy to use.*

✗ *An* easy-to-use *adhesive is easy-to-use.*

Further examples are:

a twice-weekly drama series

a sixteenth-century church

a six-cylinder engine

hassle-free travel

a walk-in bath

a no-risk, money-back guarantee

deep-sea diving

a four-wheel-drive vehicle

a not-so-tidy garden

a low-cost personal loan   *a warts-and-all biography*
a free, no-obligation quote   *dyed-in-the-wool Tories*
a left-of-centre think-tank
a one-size-fits-all solution to the problem
a dress with three-quarter-length sleeves
a junk-food-guzzling private detective
Glits is an Edinburgh-based, female-voice choir.
Our Do-It-for-You Service is safer than DIY.
Our fertilizer lasts twice as long as off-the-shelf products.
*She was packing her case in a furious, don't-anyone-dare-
argue-with-me way.*
This was noses-pressed-against-the-window journalism.

Linking with hyphens and quotation marks

Notice the use of the quotation marks and hyphens in
the following examples to link words into a single unit:

I like people with a can-do attitude.
I like people with a 'can do' attitude.
The man nodded a good-morning as I drew level.
The man nodded a 'good morning' as I drew level.

Names in compounds

Names that are not normally hyphenated remain
unhyphenated when describing a following noun, even
when some element is attached to them by a hyphen:

a Rio de Janeiro night club
a Hong Kong-born businessman
her Los Angeles-based fiancé
America's Grand Canyon-like political divisions
Bridget Jones-style single women
Thomas Hardy-esque scenes

Phrases with an added suffix

When two or more words are made to function as a single element in a sentence by the addition of a suffix (such as -*ness*), the whole compound must be hyphenated:

Esmond was being very Justice-of-the-Peace-y.
The aunts raised their eyebrows with a good deal of To-what-are-we-indebted-for-the-honour-of-this-visitness . . .

Both examples from P G Wodehouse

Phrases consisting of an adverb and an adjective or participle

The basic rule

A descriptive phrase consisting of an adverb and an adjective is not normally hyphenated:

a very silly boy
a lightly boiled egg
a cup of freshly boiled water

a quite ridiculous suggestion
a beautifully illustrated book

However, if an adverb ending in -*ly* is felt to be particularly closely linked to a following participle, it is considered acceptable by many people to have a hyphen between the two words:

a closely-written sheet of paper
a more highly-skilled and educated workforce
a legally-binding framework for compensation

While permissible, this should only be done if there really is a particular need for it, and there rarely is. It is not clear, for example, what purpose the hyphens serve here:

[x] *fondly-remembered holidays*
[x] *easily-defined genre boundaries*

As a general rule, do *not* hyphenate an adverb and a following participle.

Well, better, etc

If any of the adverbs *well, better, best, ill, worse, worst, much, little, most* and *least* plus a past participle form a phrase describing a following noun, then a hyphen is required between them:

He became one of Britain's best-loved comedy actors.
They're very well-brought-up little girls.
This is one of Hollywood's worst-kept secrets.
The tale of the ill-fated liner 'Arctic' was a sad one indeed.
Fox-hunting is a much-abused sport.
Zen calligraphy has remained a little-understood art form.
This was one of the BBC's most-watched plays.
He must be one Britain's least-trusted politicians at the moment.

No hyphen is needed when the phrase does not immediately precede a noun:

Although the book was well received, it took time for it to become popular.
A professor of medical law, he is better known to most people as a writer.

She is best known and most respected for her stand against the Iraq war.
Like every other member of the family, the house is much loved.

Every Sunday, the whole town could be seen walking through the park. There were the genuinely ✓better-off residents from the large houses round the park; there were those who desperately wanted to be thought ✗better-off because they weren't; and there were those who actually were pretty ✗badly-off but on Sundays managed to look almost as ✗well-dressed as the others.

✓ . . . there were those who desperately wanted to be thought better off because they weren't; and there were those who actually were pretty badly off but on Sundays managed to look almost as well dressed as the others.

However, compounds formed with *ill* do tend to be hyphenated even after a verb:

In my opinion, the plan was ill-conceived.
The expedition was ill-omened right from the start.
John was ill-suited to be bishop of an affluent city.

With a present participle, the tendency is to hyphenate in all positions:

She wrote a well-meaning but rather ill-informed article on unmarried motherhood.
Her suggestion was very well-meaning, I'm sure.

The same is true with other short adverbs:

The problems seem never-ending.
The study was wide-ranging and comprehensive.
My girlfriend was very long-suffering and tolerant.

It was not a puppy but a full-grown dog.
We need a harder-hitting message on drug abuse.

Adjective + noun

On occasion a hyphen may be needed to link an adjective to a following noun for the sake of clarity:

an English scholar (= a scholar who is English)
an English-scholar (= a scholar of English)

Multi-word nouns

Multi-word phrases acting as nouns are generally hyphenated:

my brother-in-law   *a man-about-town*
a jack-of-all-trades   *a jack-in-the-box*
forget-me-nots   *Johnny-come-latelys*
mothers-to-be

However, if the phrase is of the form 'X of Y' or 'X of the Y', there are no hyphens:

a Justice of the Peace   *a guard of honour*
a man of the world   *a matron of honour*
a man of action

However, compounds with special or figurative meanings are usually hyphenated:

A Portuguese man-of-war is a sort of jellyfish.

Other two-word phrases

Certain other two-word phrases need hyphens.
• Numbers from 21 to 99 and fractions should always be hyphenated:

There were forty-three of them.
Four-fifths of the population live below the official poverty line.

• A two-word phrase in which the second element is a past or present participle or a word ending in *-ed* should always be linked by a hyphen:

home-made   *short-staffed*
mind-blowing   *heart-warming*

However, some well-established compounds may be written as single words:

heartbreaking   *heartbroken*
crestfallen

• A combination of an adjective and a noun should be hyphenated:

The food in the restaurant was first-rate.
The choice of music seemed rather second-rate to me.
The job will be pretty low-level for the foreseeable future.
He bought them second-hand.

• Combinations of a noun plus an adjective are hyphenated before nouns but need not be elsewhere in a sentence:

We were wading through knee-deep mud.
Shoulder-length hair is okay by me.
It was a pitch-black night.

The mud was knee deep (or *knee-deep*).
Knee deep (or *Knee-deep*) *in mud, we were making very slow progress.*
Her hair was shoulder length (or *shoulder-length*) *and curly.*
Outside it was pitch black (or *pitch-black*).

Compound nouns formed with two elements

Usage in this area is not fixed and not totally agreed. Usage is changing and fewer hyphens are used now than before. When in doubt, consult a dictionary for the correct current hyphenation of a word.

The basic rules

In general, a compound noun is written as two separate words if it is felt that the first word simply describes the second word, but as a hyphenated word or as a single word if the compound is felt to be a single lexical unit describing a particular category of person or thing:

a bus company	*a bus-driver*
the trade balance	*a trademark*

A compound in which the first element is the object of the second element is generally hyphenated or written as a single word:

bus-driver, fox-hunting, etc
hillwalking, moneylender, etc

If the 'single lexical unit' type of word is well established and in frequent use, and if it is constructed from short words, it is likely to be written without a hyphen:

bedroom, bluebottle, goldfish, teacup, tablespoon, etc

A hyphen is more likely in longer words, though many compounds that were formerly written with a hyphen are now written without one:

dining room, food poisoning, etc

A hyphen is also frequently used to avoid an undesirable or potentially confusing juxtaposition of letters:

heart-throb rather than ✗*heartthrob*
time-exposure rather than ✗*timeexposure*

Compounds of equals

A hyphen may link words of equal status in a compound:

singer-songwriter	*secretary-treasurer*
player-manager	*actor-manager*
kilowatt-hour	*foot-pound-second*

Phrasal verbs

Phrasal verbs are combinations of simple verbs such as *get, give, put, send* or *take* with adverbs such as *in, out* or *off* or prepositions such as *for* or *with*, or both; for example:

get back, give off, kick off, knock down, pick off, put up with, warm up

Phrasal verbs should not be hyphenated:

✓ *Volunteers clean up the town.*
✓ *This event has sold out every year.*
✓ *Always allow yourself five minutes to warm up.*

✗ *British troops to move towards Baghdad to free-up US troops*
✗ *Pay-in cash or cheques to any value.*
✗ *You have to decide whether or not to contract-out.*

Nouns formed from phrasal verbs

Nouns formed from phrasal verbs are often hyphenated:

*Major clean-ups have been carried out thanks to the efforts of
local residents.*
The concert was a sell-out.
Allow yourself a five-minute warm-up.
The kick-off is at three o'clock.

Similarly:

fly-past, line-up, share-out, send-up, set-to, set-up, write-off,
etc

In some compounds the hyphen is optional (*takeaway*
or *take-away, takeover* or *take-over*) and many well-
established compounds are now usually written as
single words:

*fallout, getaway, giveaway, hangover, layabout, layout,
hideout, knockout, lookout, makeover, setback, stowaway,* etc

If the verb part of the compound has a word-ending
added to it, the compound is always hyphenated:

a grown-up, a passer-by, a hanger-on, etc
I'll need to give the house a good going-over.
I can't stand all this showing-off.
She's got a lot of growing-up to do.

Adjectives formed from phrasal verbs

Adjectives formed from phrasal verbs are hyphenated when they precede a noun:

an unhoped-for success	*her longed-for children*
a sawn-off shotgun	*a built-in fridge*
knock-down prices	*a dreadfully hung-up young man*

In other positions, current usage seems to prefer hyphenated combinations of verbs and prepositions (such as *for, of* or *with*), but unhyphenated combinations of verbs and adverbs (such as *by, in, out, past* or *up*):

His success was quite unexpected, indeed unhoped-for.
He was really hung up about what had happened.

But when the phrase is not felt to be acting as an adjective, no hyphen is needed:

Children had been longed for and tried for for many years.

Hyphens with prefixes, suffixes and other word-forming elements

The basic rules

In general, hyphens are not used with prefixes (*un-, dis-, mis-, pre-, re-,* etc), suffixes (*-ly, -ness, -ful, -dom,* etc) or word-forming elements (*electro-, hydro-, photo-, -itis, -lysis,* etc).

A hyphen is correctly used to avoid the juxtaposition of identical letters, especially vowels:

re-enter, pre-eclampsia, electro-optics, anti-inflammatory, bell-like, cross-stitch

In some cases compounds without hyphens are acceptable:

cooperate, reenact, etc

(When in doubt, follow your dictionary.)

A hyphen is used to distinguish words that would otherwise be identical:

re-cover = 'cover again', and *recover* = 'get better'
re-count = 'count again' and *recount* = 'tell'
co-op and *coop*

A hyphen is used to clarify the structure of uncommon words:

Many of the animals in the abattoir had been mis-stunned.
Pensions were often 'mis-sold' (a euphemism for fraud).
He was being unbearably kind and understanding and . . . just uncle-ish.
Here and there in the crowd there were a few beardless and moustache-less youths.

Prefixes

If *un-* is added to a word beginning with a capital letter, the new word is usually hyphenated: *un-American, un-Islamic,* etc. But it is now acceptable, though much less common, to write such words without hyphens: *unChristian,* etc.

Ex-, non- and *pro-* are usually followed by hyphens:

ex-wife, non-flammable, pro-life

But note *nonconformist, nondescript, nonentity, nonplus, nonsense*.

When *ex-* precedes two or more words that form a single unit of meaning in a sentence, it should be linked to the first word with a hyphen, but the other words remain unhyphenated:

an ex-Los Angeles policeman
the ex-Bay City Rollers drummer

However, if linking *ex-* to the following word produces something awkward or potentially confusing, rephrase the sentence (for example using 'former' instead of *ex-*):

☒ *an ex-public toilet* (is this now a private toilet?)
✓ *a former public toilet*

A hyphen may be inserted when a prefix is added to a word that is itself hyphenated (though sometimes neither option looks quite right):

an unre-covered or *an un-re-covered seat*

And occasionally more than one hyphen may be needed:

an anti-high-tariff campaign

Long-established words beginning with *co-* are now usually not hyphenated:

coefficient, cooperate, coordinate, etc

Newer coinages, on the other hand, are likely to be hyphenated:

co-agent, co-author, co-chair, co-driver, co-educational, etc

To avoid confusion, write *co-op* and *co-opt* rather than
✗*coop* and **✗***coopt*, but *coed* is correct.

Suffixes
Suffixes are generally not preceded by hyphens. However, for clarity it may sometimes be better to hyphenate:

sheer pie-in-the-sky-ism
a hail-fellow-well-met-ish sort of guy
Bringing in identity cards seems excessive to me, a bit sledge-hammer-to-crack-a-nut-ish.
She was Botoxed or Botox-ed to the eyeballs.
We have always fetishized or fetish-ized female bodies.
She waved a cigarette-ed hand towards the baby.

Word-forming elements
Anti- is not normally followed by a hyphen:

anticlockwise, antifreeze, etc

But some words are hyphenated (especially one-off coinages):

anti-hero, anti-marketeer, etc
Bridget is neurotic, smug, anti-smug, conscious of every ounce of cellulite.

When in doubt, follow your dictionary.

  -itis is often used facetiously to designate supposed diseases. Usually no hyphen is needed, but there may be one following a vowel:

Arnie has footballitis, a disease that afflicts millions of men.
Don't phone me, as I have phone-itis.

Strictly speaking, *mid-* is a word-forming element like *anti-* or *contra-*. It should therefore be linked to the following word with a hyphen:

This started in the mid-1970s.
Two English Songs of the Mid-15th Century
From mid-May to mid-June, the Mozarts stayed in Naples.
I am in the mid-course of my life.
By mid-afternoon many people were evidently hungry.

There is a trend nowadays towards treating *mid* as a word in its own right with omission of the hyphen:

Imported cloth became more difficult to obtain from the mid 1980s.
The record stopped in mid tune.

At present, however, hyphenated forms are still preferable, with certain exceptions:

When *mid* occurs parallel to another word that does not require a hyphen, the hyphen is best omitted:

Carrie is in her mid to late twenties.
This went on through the late third and mid to late fourth centuries AD.
Terrorist attacks increased by over 20 per cent between mid July and early August.

In some cases, e.g. certain place-names, a hyphen is not correct:

He had travelled there from his home in Mid Glamorgan.

Words formed with *self-* are hyphenated unless the second element is a suffix:

self-control, self-help but *selfless*

Compounds formed with *half-* are usually hyphenated:

half-baked, half-term, etc but *halfway, halfwit, halfpenny*

Words formed with *-like* are usually hyphenated unless they are well established:

grass-like, ostrich-like but *childlike, ladylike*

Miscellaneous points

• When referring to a prefix, suffix or word-forming element, it is correct but not necessary to add a hyphen:

Consider the suffix '-ism'.

• Logically there should be a hyphen in *no-one*:

anybody : anyone   *everybody : everyone*
somebody : someone

so:

nobody : no-one (with a hyphen added to separate the two o's)

Unfortunately, language is not always logical, and the most common spelling nowadays is *no one* (although *no-one* is also correct).

   Do not write ✗ *noone* as a single word.

• Note the correct hyphenation of *wild-goose chase* (= 'hunt for wild geese'), *fine-tooth comb* (= 'comb with fine teeth'). *Fine toothcomb* is also considered correct by many (but not all) authorities. *Fine-toothed comb* must have the hyphen between *fine* and *toothed*.

Frequently lost hyphens

When two or more hyphenated words occur together in a sentence and have some part in common, the part they have in common may be omitted:

full-time and part-time staff > full- and part-time staff
fifteen-year-olds and sixteen-year-olds > fifteen- and sixteen-year-olds
servicemen and servicewomen > servicemen and -women

In all such cases, the hyphen preceding or following the omitted part must be retained, as in the above examples. Errors in this respect are frequent and varied; for example:

✗ *full and part-time staff*
✗ *full and part time staff*
✗ *14 and 15-year-olds*
✗ *14-15 year olds*
✗ *servicemen and women*
✗ *pre and post-war Britain*
✗ *smudge and water-resistant.*

Note the difference between, for example, *her brother and sister-in-law* (= 'her brother and her sister-in-law') and *her brother- and sister-in-law* (= 'her brother-in-law and her sister-in-law').

Word-splitting hyphens

It is sometimes necessary to split a word at the end of a line. If you are working on a word-processor, this may be done automatically (though many word-processors are programmed to avoid word splits altogether); if you are writing by hand, you have to make your own decision about where to split.

There is often more than one place in which a word may be split correctly. As a general rule, try to split a word between any two of its basic structural elements:

broadminded > broad-minded or *broadmind-ed*
excitement > excite-ment or *ex-citement*
misunderstood > mis-understood or *misunder-stood*
collective > collect-ive or *col-lective*
expensive > expens-ive or *ex-pensive*
geophysics > geo-physics
prepare > pre-pare
occur > oc-cur

When letters are doubled in forming nouns or participles, split between the doubled letters:

swim-ming, run-ner, prefer-red

Where there is no obvious grammatical structure to the word, split at a suitable pronounceable point between syllables. If there is only one consonant, make the split before it:

thou-sand, trou-sers, etc

If there is more than one consonant, split between two consonants or after the first consonant of a group of three:

mur-der, spec-trum, dol-drums, etc

Never split a word in such a way that the part at the end of the line misleads the reader as to what is coming:

fastidious > ✓fas-tidious not *✗fast-idious*
reinstall > ✓re-install not *✗rein-stall*
therapist > ✓ther-apist not *✗the-rapist*
represent > ✓rep-resent not *✗re-present*

The split should suggest the pronunciation of the word:

✓spe-cial not *✗spec-ial*
✓dep-recate not *✗de-precate*
✓rep-resent not *✗re-present*
✓aristoc-racy but *✓aristo-cratic*
✓bureauc-racy but *✓bureau-cratic*
✓psycho-linguistic but *✓psychol-ogy*

Do not split words between letters that together represent a single sound, such as *th, ch, sh,* etc:

✓teach-er not *✗teac-her*

. . . nor between letters if one of them is silent:

✓plumb-er not *✗plum-ber*

Do not split words of one syllable:

✓wash-ing but not *✗wash-ed*
✓invent-ed

(Some people feel that having only two letters carried over is undesirable.)

Do not split personal names.

Split a hyphenated compound word at an already existing hyphen. Do not split the word at the end of a line in such a way as to require a further word-splitting hyphen:

✗*space-sav-ing*
✗*ill-con-ceived*
✗*fifteenth-cen-tury*
✗*chardonnay-swig-ging*

If you want more help with hyphenation, either choose a dictionary that shows how to hyphenate words or else buy a special hyphenation dictionary (of which there are several available in shops).

Special effects

Hyphenation may be used to represent stammering or slow speech:

'You k-kissed B-B-Bethan?' she said, both amazed and horrified.
'B-but B-Bethan's a c-c-cow!'
Say it again please, s-l-o-w-l-y.
I want to go to Keynsham. That's K-e-y-n-sh-a-m, near Bristol.

Summary of key points

- Two or more words that have to be understood as single elements in a sentence are generally hyphenated.
- Phrases formed with *well, better, best, ill, worse, worst, most* and *least* plus a past participle require a hyphen before a noun but (with the exception of *ill*) not elsewhere.
- Multi-word phrases acting as nouns are generally hyphenated, but hyphenation in two-word compound nouns is unpredictable.
- Phrasal verbs should not be hyphenated, but nouns and adjectives formed from phrasal verbs usually are.
- When two or more hyphenated words occur together in a sentence and have some part in common, the part they have in common may be omitted but the hyphen preceding or following the omitted part must be retained.
- When splitting a word at the end of a line, make the split at a structurally or phonetically suitable place, and never where it could confuse the reader.

17
Capital letters

'The collection of ballads will in future be reserved for
private study, with the object of making poetry
tributary' – Wegg was so proud of having found this
word, that he said it again, with a capital letter –
'Tributary, to friendship.'

Charles Dickens, *Our Mutual Friend*

Capitals in sentences

The basic rule
A sentence must begin with a capital letter:

The girl took some keys out of her bag.
We hated the cook's soggy pastry.
What are you doing?
My goodness! What a surprise!

If a sentence is a comment enclosed in brackets, it does
not begin with a capital letter, but if there is more than
one sentence in the brackets, all but the first do begin
with a capital letter:

*I untied his hands (that was my big mistake) and before I knew
it he had grabbed the knife.*

I untied his hands (that was my big mistake. I'll know better next time) and before I knew it he had grabbed the knife.

A short question included in a larger sentence may have but need not have a capital letter:

The question 'what now?' is one that no-one in the Middle East can answer confidently.
The question 'What now?' is one that no-one in the Middle East can answer confidently.

Direct speech

Sentences quoted in direct speech begin with a capital letter:

She said quietly, 'He's left me.'

If the sentence is split, the second part does not begin with a capital:

'You both know,' she said, 'what you have to do.'

When direct speech is written without quotation marks, it may, or equally well may not, begin with a capital letter:

I thought to myself, Why me?
You may ask, what is our aim?

Quotations

If a full-sentence quotation is grammatically integrated into your sentence, for example by means of a linking word such as 'that', it is correct to replace the initial capital letter of the sentence with a lower-case letter (although some authorities prefer the capital letter to be retained in this position):

✓ *Drummond states that 'the Egyptian attack brought renewed crisis to the kingdom, with a number of minor principalities asserting their independence'.*

✓ *Drummond states that 'The Egyptian attack brought renewed crisis to the kingdom, with a number of minor principalities asserting their independence'.*

If a full-sentence quotation is not integrated into your sentence by means of a linking word, it should retain the capital letter:

As George Mikes once said, 'An Englishman, even if he is alone, forms an orderly queue of one.'

If the quotation is not itself a complete sentence, there should be no capital letter:

George Mikes once said that an Englishman, even if he is alone, 'forms an orderly queue of one'.

Poetry

In traditional poetry, each line begins with a capital letter whether or not it is the beginning of a sentence:

There was no leaf upon the forest bare,
   No flower upon the ground,
And little motion in the air
   Except the mill-wheel's sound.

Percy Bysshe Shelley, 'Archy's Song'

In modern poetry, this may not be the case. There may not even be capital letters marking the beginnings of grammatically separate sentences:

I said to her
do not go
you'll only be trapped
and bewitched
and will suffer in vain.

Miroslav Holub, 'The Cat'

Names

The basic rule

Capitals are required for the first letter of names. Any person or thing with a unique name requires the first letter of that name, and of all the main words of the name, to be a capital; for example:

- people, gods, animals, etc:

Peter	*Lucy*	*Tony Blair*
God	*Odin*	*Ptah*
Red Rum	*Bugs Bunny*	

. . . adjectives derived from names:

Edwardian	*Kafkaesque*	*Shakespearian*
Benedictine	*Franciscan*	

. . . and other words derived from names:

Thatcherism	*Blairite*	*Britneyfication*

- ethnic groups:

Picts   Sioux   Xhosa
Black Americans   Native Americans

. . . and related adjectives:

Pictish   Siouan

- places:

Paris   England   Cornwall
Barnton Road   Waterloo Station   Loch Lomond
Mount Everest

. . . languages:

Italian   Welsh   Esperanto

. . . related adjectives and nouns:

American   French   Glaswegian

. . . and other derived words:

Americanize Frenchify

- days of the week and months of the year:

Monday   April

- festivals:

Christmas   Easter   Wesak
Diwali   Hanukkah   May Day

- religions:

Buddhism   Christianity   Islam
Hinduism   Sikhism   Catholicism

. . . and related nouns and adjectives:

Buddhist	*Christian*	*Muslim*
Sikh	*Hindu*	*Catholic*

• organizations:

British Aerospace	*Oxford University Press*

• periods and events of history:

the Ice Age	*the Renaissance*
the Russian Revolution	

• acts of parliament, etc:

the Corn Laws	*the Declaration of Independence*

Minor words

Notice that in all the above categories, minor words such as *the* and *of* are not capitalized:

Winnie the Pooh	*Vlad the Impaler*
the Bay of Biscay	*the River Thames*
the Sea of Azov	*the Pyrenees*
Newcastle upon Tyne	*Carlton-on-Trent*
Ashford in the Water	*Weston-super-Mare*
the Church of Scotland	*Action on Smoking and Health*

However, in names that specifically include 'the' as part of the name, 'the' may correctly be written with a capital *T* even in the middle of a sentence:

These kids find The Salvation Army is ready to accept them.
They have an office in The Hague.
Morrissey used to sing with The Smiths.

If the name of a newspaper or magazine is already highlighted within the sentence, it is correct to leave the word 'the' unhighlighted and not capitalize it:

✓ *He wrote a letter to The Times but it wasn't published.*
✓ *He wrote a letter to the* Times *but it wasn't published.*

In personal names of foreign origin, minor words such as *de* and *von* or *van* are usually not capitalized, but usage varies and you must simply spell names the way the people themselves spell or spelt them:

the Venus de Milo	*the Marquis de Sade*
Walter de la Mare	*Daphne Du Maurier*
Leonardo da Vinci	*Baron von Richthofen*
Ludwig van Beethoven	*Vincent van Gogh*
Martin Van Buren	*Sir Anthony Van Dyck*

In names beginning with *Mac* and *Mc*, the following letter may be a capital letter, or it may not:

MacDonald	*McEnroe*
Macleod	*Mackenzie*

Here again you must simply spell names the way the people themselves spell or spelt them.

In Irish names, *O* is always capitalized, and followed by a capital:

O'Brien	*O'Neill*

Words derived from names

Many words which are in origin people's names or which are derived from names, but which have lost their close association with the people concerned, do not take a capital letter:

wellingtons (named after the Duke of Wellington)
sandwich (named after the Earl of Sandwich)
watt (named after James Watt)
ampere (named after Louis Ampère)
pasteurize (from Louis Pasteur)
bowdlerize (from Thomas Bowdler)
boycott (from Charles Boycott)

Both *Platonic love* and *platonic love* are correct. Similarly *Herculean* and *herculean*, but only *quixotic*. You write *Bible*, *Gospel*, *Messiah* and *Scripture* but *biblical*, *gospel* (as an adjective), *messianic*, and *scriptural*.

● -isms

'-isms' are written with an initial small letter unless they are based on a word that begins with a capital letter:

communism, existentialism, fascism, etc
Kantianism, Maoism, Marxism, etc

Personification

When abstract nouns are treated as people, for example in poetry, they are given capital letters:

When Love with unconfined wings
  Hovers within my gates . . .

Richard Lovelace, 'To Althea from Prison'

I love waves, and winds, and storms,
  Everything almost
Which is Nature's, . . .

Percy Bysshe Shelley, 'Invocation'

Brand names

Strictly speaking, capital letters are required with all proprietary names: *Hoover, Rollerblades, Xerox,* etc. When words like these come to be used as general terms for the objects they denote and the activities they are used for, without implying the use of products of particular companies, they are usually written without capitals: *hoover, rollerblade, xerox.*

Companies strongly deprecate the use of their trademarks and brand names as generic terms written without capital letters, as this threatens their trademark status. So although it is perfectly normal not to use capitals for words like *hoover* in informal writing, you should in formal and technical writing be careful to use a capital letter with any word that is a trademark or brand name. Check in a dictionary: all such words should be marked with an ® or have some other indicator of their proprietary status.

The capital is optional when these words are used as verbs.

Planets and stars

Planet and star names are written with capital letters:

Jupiter   *Mars*   *Alpha Centauri*

The words *sun, moon* and *earth* need not be capitalized, but they can be:

The moon orbits the earth.
The Earth is made up of several different layers.

When it is used alongside other planet names, write *Earth*:

Like Earth, Venus and Mercury, Mars is a rocky planet.

In idioms, do not use capitals:

What on earth are you doing?
He was over the moon about it.

Countries, regions and towns

Names of countries and regions require capital letters:

  the Middle East   *South Africa*

But a word that is not actually part of the name of a definite place does not require a capital letter:

  central London   *southern Africa*

Therefore it is correct to write

the Republic of South Africa (the name of the country)

but

South Africa is a republic.

Similarly:

They live in the south of France.

but

They live in the South. ('the South' being understood as a definite area)

Words denoting places of origin

Words relating to places are written with capital letters:

German sausages   *French wines*

This is true even if the words no longer imply a real relationship with a place:

Danish pastries   *French windows*
Brussels sprouts   *Cheddar cheese*
Cornish pasties   *Dutch courage*

Some people write *danish pastries, french windows*, etc, but most authorities still prefer the capital letters.

Both *plaster of Paris* and *plaster of paris* are correct.

Titles

Words that are used in titles should begin with capital letters:

the Prime Minister   *the Archbishop of*
                             Canterbury
Sir Bernard Lyons   *Baroness Thatcher*
the Prophet Muhammad   *the Three Musketeers*
Queen Mary   *the President of the United*
                             States
Parliament   *the Government*

The same words do not, of course, require capitals when they are not being used in titles:

How many prime ministers have there been since Disraeli?
There have been two English queens with the name of Elizabeth.
Scotland has its own parliament.

Saint Jude is the patron saint of hopeless causes.
He knows a lot about Norse gods and goddesses.

When a title is hyphenated, both parts should have capital letters:

Major-General Gordon
Vice-President Cheney

Titles of books, plays, etc

All the main words (the nouns, pronouns, verbs, adjectives and adverbs) in the title of a book, play, film, etc must begin with a capital letter, whereas the minor words (the articles *the* and *a/an*, prepositions and conjunctions) should not have capitals. Nonetheless, the first and last words in a title must always begin with a capital letter:

I'm looking for a book called 'The Men and the Girls'.
You really must read 'Freedom in a Rocking Boat'.
Who sang 'It's My Party and I'll Cry if I Want To'?

However, practice varies: some people will begin 'and' and 'or' with lower-case letters, but capitalize other conjunctions; others recommend writing prepositions and conjunctions of four or more letters with initial capital letters but shorter words with initial lower-case letters. Whatever rule you adopt, be consistent.

If there is a hyphenated compound in a title, both parts may be written with initial capital letters:

Chapter 3 is called 'The Self-Exciting System'.
Have you got a copy of 'Managing the Non-Profit Organization'?

There is a more recent school of thought, especially in academic circles, that prefers only the first words in book titles, etc to have capitals:

One of your set books for this term is 'Freedom in a rocking boat'.

Unless you are specifically required to follow this practice, you should keep to the traditional style with capitals for all the important words.

Seasons

The names of seasons are not usually written with capital letters (thus: *winter, summer, autumn*), but it is correct to write *Spring* if necessary for the sake of clarity.

Subjects of study

Subjects of study are not normally written with initial capital letters:

We've got two periods of maths this morning, then two periods of chemistry.

However, the name of the subject may require a capital letter on other grounds:

Have we got French today?

However, when a subject of study is part of the title of a course, degree, etc, it should be written with a capital letter:

She's got a BSc in Physics and the Philosophy of Science.

Abbreviations and symbols

Abbreviations and symbols that consist of a single letter may be either capital letters or lower-case letters:

A (= 'ampere' or 'answer'), *C* (= 'Celsius'), *F* (= 'Fahrenheit'), etc

a (= 'acre'), *c* (= 'carat'), *f* (= 'fathom'), etc

If you are not sure whether to use a capital letter or a lower-case letter, check in a dictionary.

Abbreviations consisting of the initial letters of two or more words are usually written completely in capital letters:

AGM, *APR* (= 'annual percentage rate'), *BA*, *BBC*, *MOT*, *NUM*, *PLC*, *PS* (= 'postscript'), *TLC* (= 'tender loving care'), *USA*, *WSW* (= 'west-south-west'), etc

When an abbreviation takes in more than the first letter of a word, only the first letter is a capital:

BSc (= 'Bachelor of Science'), *PhD* or *DPhil* (= 'Doctor of Philosophy')

The abbreviations of the names of some organizations, etc have become established as names and are pronounced as single words. In such cases, the names may be spelt entirely in capital letters or with only an initial capital:

NATO or *Nato*, *UNESCO* or *Unesco*, *AIDS* or *Aids*, etc

Some abbreviations of this type are now so well established in the language that they are never written with capital letters:

radar (= 'radio detection and ranging')
sonar (= 'sound navigation and ranging')

In the abbreviated forms of the names of some organizations that have 'of' or 'for' in their name, the 'of' and 'for' may be abbreviated to a capital letter or a lowercase letter. In such cases, follow the practice of the organization concerned:

FoE or FOE (= 'Friends of the Earth')
DfES (= 'Department for Education and Skills')
DFID (= 'Department for International Development')

A few abbreviations may be written with lower-case letters:

AGM or *agm, AKA* or *aka* (= 'also known as'), *BCG* or *bcg, PLC* or *plc*

Some abbreviations are always (or nearly always) written with lower-case letters:

asap (= 'as soon as possible'), *fob* (= 'free on board'), *gbh* (= 'grievous bodily harm')

Abbreviations of Latin words are written in lower-case letters:

a.m., p.m., e.g., i.e., viz.

Symbols and abbreviations for weights and measures are written in lower-case letters:

in., cm, mph, etc

The first (or only) letter of the symbol for a chemical element is written as a capital letter:

Common salt is sodium chloride, NaCl.
Water is H_2O.

Post codes are written with capital letters, as are American zip (or ZIP) codes:

Edinburgh EH14 6JJ
South Dakota SD 57301

Other uses of capital letters
• 'Topping and tailing' letters
You write *Dear Sir, My dear Frances,* etc at the start of a letter, and at the end you write *Yours sincerely* or *Yours faithfully*.

• Emphasis
Capital letters are often used for emphasis:

Since I have given you all this advice, I add this crowning precept, the most valuable of all: NEVER TAKE ANYBODY'S ADVICE.

George Bernard Shaw, *Advice to a Young Critic*

The use of capital letters for emphasis is acceptable in informal writing, but in formal writing this is better done with italics or boldface (and done sparingly):

If you want a HOT DEAL, call us now for a free estimate. Remember: YOU PAY NOTHING until your conservatory is completed to your satisfaction.

A similar use of capitals for emphasis may sometimes be seen in advertisements and headlines:

Probably the Biggest Manufacturer of Quality Sheds in Scotland
Now I Can Play a Bigger Part in My Kids' Education – Thanks to
Home-Ed Books
Radical Cleric to Face UK Terror Charges

A humorous use of capitals for emphasis in informal writing can be seen in the following examples:

James I slobbered at the mouth and had favourites; he was thus a Bad King.

W C Sellar and R J Yeatman, 1066 and All That

Owl hasn't exactly got Brain, but he Knows Things.

A A Milne, Winnie-the-Pooh

German nouns

In German, all nouns are written with capital letters. When these words are borrowed into English, they are generally still written with capital letters:

Gastarbeiter, Lebensraum, Schadenfreude, Weltanschauung, Weltschmerz

However, as such words become absorbed into English, they tend to lose their capitals; thus:

blitzkrieg, festschrift, kitsch, lederhosen, leitmotiv, lieder, realpolitik, sauerkraut, wunderkind

There is no clear ruling about which German nouns fall into which category, and authorities differ. Follow your own dictionary.

Pronouns

I is always written with a capital letter.

Pronouns used to address or refer to God and Jesus are generally written with initial capital letters, though less so than formerly:

God has power over all things and He is able to do everything. All His creatures depend on Him for all they need.

Small capitals

If possible, *AD* and *BC* should be written with small capitals:

Caesar invaded Britain in 55 BC.

If for some reason you cannot write or print small capitals, use ordinary capital letters:

Caesar invaded Britain in 55 BC.

Summary of key points

- Sentences begin with capital letters.
- Quotations only require capital letters if they are complete sentences and are not grammatically integrated into a larger sentence.
- Names and titles require capital letters. But the names of common objects and activities named after people do not need capitals.
- The first words and all the main words of the title of a book, film, play, etc should begin with capital letters.
- Many abbreviations and symbols are written with capital letters, but not the symbols for units of measurement.
- German nouns used in English may or may not be written with capital letters.

18
Paragraphs

At the end of a long and boring road I came upon a paragraph which was high, rich, soaring to the clouds.

Michel de Montaigne (French philosopher)

It is beyond the scope of this book to teach you how to write paragraphs that your reader will look on as high, rich and soaring to the clouds, but whether your writing is soaring or boring, there are one or two things you should know about paragraphs.

A paragraph is a piece of written text consisting of one or more sentences that relate to a common topic. Any piece of writing more than a few sentences in length is normally broken up into paragraphs, as this makes it easier to read than a long, unbroken text.

Indenting paragraphs

Paragraphs are usually indented slightly to the right (up to five letter spaces, but often less). But *not all* paragraphs are indented. The *first* paragraph in a chapter, article, report, etc is not indented, nor is the first paragraph after a section heading or subheading. (In addition, some people prefer not to indent a new paragraph that immediately follows a table, an illustration or anything else that breaks up the page, but in general it is better to indent in order to indicate that it *is* a new paragraph and not simply a continuation of the preceding one.) If paragraphs on a page are separated by blank lines, then they are not indented.

The rule is, simply, that you only indent a paragraph if the indenting is the only clear way of showing that that is where a new paragraph begins. If the beginning of a paragraph is shown in any other way, then you do not indent.

Speech

In direct speech in novels and stories, each speaker's words begin as a new paragraph and are indented. But here again, the paragraph is not indented if it comes at the beginning of a separate section of the text.

19

Italics, boldface type and underlining

The man who uses italics is like the man who raises his voice in conversation and talks loudly in order to make himself heard.

Herbert Henry Asquith

Just as the orator marks his good things by a dramatic pause, or by raising and lowering his voice, or by gesture, so the writer marks his epigrams with italics, setting the little gem, so to speak, like a jeweller.

Oscar Wilde, in reply to Asquith

Italics are perhaps not much used in everyday life to draw attention to epigrams, but they are used, as Oscar Wilde used them, to draw the reader's attention to something in a passage of writing. Boldface type and underlining are used for the same purpose, as are quotation marks.

Examples in this book are written in italics. But in order to explain the correct use of italics, the examples in *this* chapter are in the same print as normal text, so that examples of italics in use are actually in italics.

Italics

Highlighting
Italics are one way of picking out a word or phrase in a sentence:

The word *existentialism* has not been popular in some circles. There are two *t*'s in *bottle*.

This kind of highlighting can also be done with quotation marks:

When some writers talk of 'personalism', what they have in mind is a type of philosophy not much different from existentialism.

Emphasis
Italic type is used to pick out a word or phrase to show that it is being emphasized:

Now I'm *really* annoyed with you!
Human beings are *thinking* animals. We *learn*. We *adapt*. That's how we survive.
That one? Why on earth do you want *that* one?

Contrast

Italic type is used to pick out elements of a sentence that are being contrasted:

Why do we write 'eat*able*' but 'ed*ible*'?

Foreign words and phrases

Foreign words and phrases are printed in italic type:

It's not true that immigrants are arriving at Dover *en masse*.
The man's hair was cut *en brosse*.
I didn't have time to build a proper hide, so *faute de mieux* I covered myself with branches.

Words of foreign origin which have become accepted as English words are not written in italics:

Do you want spaghetti or macaroni tonight?
I wasn't arguing a priori, but from empirical evidence.

Obviously this is a grey area. (Some people would want to italicize 'a priori' in the last example, some would not.) If you are not sure whether or not a word is now fully accepted as an English word, check in a dictionary: some dictionaries (though not all) show whether the editors think a word should be in italics or not. But in any case, any foreign word whose meaning you have to explain should certainly be in italics.

Abbreviations of Latin words and phrases that are in common use, such as *i.e.*, *e.g.* and *etc*, should not be italicized:

We are looking for old drawings, photos, stamps, magazine articles, books, etc.

Titles and names

The titles of books, newspapers, magazines, films, plays, long poems, television programmes, etc and the names of ships, aircraft, spacecraft, etc are often put in italic print:

Nearly five years ago, Helen Fielding published *Bridget Jones: The Edge of Reason*, a sequel to the enormously successful *Bridget Jones's Diary*.

In 1938, Sartre wrote the novel *La Nausée* ('Nausea').

I'm sure I read that in last month's *Reader's Digest*.

He went on to summarize the teaching of the encyclical *Humani Generis*.

The ship was called the *Mary Rose*.

You do not, however, italicize the Bible, the books of the Bible, the Qur'an, and other scriptures.

Quotation marks can be used instead of italics, but if possible use italics. Notice that in the Sartre example, as also in the 'eatable/edible' example above, it can be useful to use both italics *and* quotation marks for highlighting.

Chapters of books, articles in journals, songs, short poems and stories are by convention put in quotation marks:

For more about this, see Lakoff's article 'A Note on Vagueness and Ambiguity' in *Linguistic Inquiry*.

Scientific names

Species and genus names are written in italic:

The blackbird (*Turdus merula*) is a member of the thrush family.

Higher-ranking scientific names (class, order, etc) are not written in italics.

Roman for italic

If for some reason your text is already in italics, highlight your words in non-italic type:

She didn't want to give him *carte blanche*.
She didn't want to give him carte blanche.

Underlining

You use underlining in handwritten texts where you would use italics in a printed text.

Boldface type

Like italics, boldface type (or bold type) can be use for highlighting and emphasis:

History changed on October 4, 1957, when the Soviet Union successfully launched **Sputnik I**.
If you want a **hot deal**, don't delay. Phone us now on 09876 543210.

Boldface is also frequently used for titles and headings.

20
Direct speech, correspondence, and essays and reports

Direct speech

The punctuation of direct speech has been discussed in various chapters of this book. For convenience, the main points are gathered together here.

- Direct speech is written inside quotation marks:

'Do you need all that?' asked Agnes.

Quotation marks are not necessary round direct speech when the words quoted are a person's thoughts or a rhetorical question:

Why me? he asked himself.

If the words quoted are not the *exact* words that a person said or thought, there cannot be quotation marks:

'Where are they going?' he wondered.
Where were they going? he wondered.

When direct speech is written without quotation marks, it may, or equally well may not, begin with a capital letter:

I thought to myself, Why me?
You may ask, what is our aim?

• British English prefers single quotation marks:

'I'll be back,' said Arnie.

Double quotation marks are preferred in American English:

"I'll be back," said Arnie.

Double quotation marks are acceptable in British English and are the usual form of quotation marks in handwritten texts.

• Punctuation marks are placed inside the quotation marks:

'What does your dog look like?' she asked.

• When a speech verb follows a statement, the full stop at the end of the statement is replaced by a comma:

'I don't think that's very funny,' she said.

Other punctuation marks are not replaced by a comma:

'What was that noise?' she whispered.
'Look out!' he shouted.

A dash that marks an uncompleted sentence is not followed by a comma:

'Give me that back, or I'll –' he said.

• When a sentence in direct speech is split by a verb of speaking, there is a comma after the verb, and the continuation of the sentence begins with a small letter:

'There are,' she said, *'a lot of changes to be made round here.'*

There is also a comma at the split in the sentence, placed inside the quotation marks:

'There are,' she said, *'a lot of changes to be made round here.'*

When what follows the verb is a new sentence, there is a full stop after the verb and the new sentence begins with a capital letter:

'There are a lot of changes to be made round here,' she said. *'We'll start tomorrow.'*

• When a speech verb precedes direct speech, it is generally followed by a comma, although it is not wrong to omit the comma:

She turned to him and said, 'I hate you.'

A colon may be used instead of a comma, but a colon makes a rather emphatic introduction to speech, and is therefore mostly used in formal, solemn or dramatic contexts.

When a passage of direct speech stands in the middle of a sentence, there should be no colon or comma, as this would disrupt the structure of the sentence:

As the result was announced, she screamed 'Oh, my God' and
began to shake.

• When the end of a passage of direct speech coincides
with the end of a sentence, and there should logically be
two punctuation marks, when the second punctuation
mark would have been a full stop, it is omitted:

Some child behind me was whining, 'I'm bored.'
The farmer shouted to us, 'Don't let them get out!'
I said, 'What did you say to me?'

If one of the punctuation marks is a question mark
and the other is an exclamation mark, neither is
dropped:

Why did you shout, 'Look out!'?
Stop saying, 'Why? Why? Why?'!

If the two punctuation marks are both question marks,
they may both be kept, but generally one or other of
them is dropped:

Why did she say, 'Who are you?'?
Why did she say, 'Who are you?'
Why did she say, 'Who are you'?

Do not drop a question mark that is the only indication
that a sentence is a question:

And then she said, 'He isn't dead?'

• In novels and stories, each speaker's words begin as
a new paragraph.

   If a passage of direct speech goes beyond a single
paragraph, each new paragraph should start with an

opening quotation mark, but only the final paragraph should have a closing quotation mark.

Correspondence

Addresses
No commas are required in addresses:

John Brown
5 Cedar Grove
Barnton
ST5 6HU

Nor do addresses need to have a progressive rightward indentation, though there is nothing actually wrong with this (and it is still preferred by some people):

John Brown
  5 Cedar Grove
    Barnton
      SY15 6HU

At the top of a letter, your address usually goes to the right-hand side of the page and the address of the person you are writing to goes at the left-hand margin.

Salutation and complimentary close
A comma is still usually written after 'Dear Sir, etc' at the beginning of a letter and 'Yours faithfully, etc' at the end, though there are some authorities who now consider this unnecessary.

In American usage, the salutation in a business letter is followed by a colon, but by a comma in informal letters.

Dates

There are now usually no commas in dates:

5 July 2004 but *July 5, 2004*

The date should go below your address. There may be a blank line between them.

Emails

Emails written in an informal style may use punctuation different from that normally found even in informal letters. For example, the salutation may be followed by an exclamation mark or a colon:

Hi Norah!
Thanks for your email. . . .

John:
Thanks for your email. . . .

This seems unexceptionable, but in more formal emails keep to the traditional punctuation:

Dear Mrs Brown,
Thank you for your email. . . .

Essays and reports

Titles

• Like newspaper headlines, the titles of essays and reports are not punctuated with full stops. Any other punctuation marks, such as question marks to indicate questions, should be used as normal.

If typed or printed, titles are usually centred on the page, in letters larger than the size of the text print, and in boldface type. In handwritten essays, the title is generally written starting at the left-hand margin, in the same size of letter as the text itself, and underlined.

If there is both a title and a subtitle, there should be a colon at the end of the title:

Existentialism: Its Contribution to the Lyrics of Lennon and McCartney

The title and subtitle can be on the same line or, especially if they are both quite long, on separate lines:

Existentialist Thought in Mid-20th-Century Liverpool Graffiti: Its Contribution to the Lyrics of Lennon and McCartney

• There are two accepted styles for capital letters in titles. In one, all the main words in the title begin with a capital letter, while the minor words do not:

America's Contribution to World Peace at the Beginning of the 21st Century

Another style has only the first word in a title beginning with a capital letter:

America's contribution to world peace at the beginning of the 21st century

However, even if the first word in a title is a minor word, it should always be capitalized, and in the first style, the same applies to the last word. Any other word that requires a capital letter by the normal rules of English spelling should of course have one in either style of title.

Section headings

• Section headings should be text-size, in boldface type if printed and underlined if handwritten. If there are many sections in the essay or report (and especially if there are subsections as well), it may be best to number the sections.

Section and subsection headings begin at the left-hand margin. A heading is usually placed on a separate line and followed by a blank line:

3. International Aid

Much was expected of international aid, but much that has been funded by it has been less than a total success. . . .

The title should not be followed by a full stop or colon, but other punctuation may be used as required. If a heading comes in two parts, it may be punctuated with a colon, in the same style as for titles above.

Alternatively, the title may be placed at the beginning of the first paragraph of the section, in which case it ends with a full stop:

3. International Aid. *Much was expected of international aid but much that has been funded by it has been less than a total success. . . .*

• If there are subsections in the essay or report as well as sections, you will almost certainly have to number them so that your reader can keep track of which subsections belong together. Put each heading on a separate line, preferably separated by a blank line. The text can start on a separate line or run on from a subsection heading as in the two styles described above.

A good way of numbering sections and subsections is as follows:

3. International Aid

3.1 Early Days

3.1.1 The British Contribution

3.1.2 Criticisms of the British Contribution to International Aid

3.2 . . .

If it is necessary to have smaller paragraphs or sections set apart, you can use letters of the alphabet or roman numerals.

Paragraphs

The first paragraph after a title or a heading that stands on a separate line is not indented, but all following paragraphs are. If all paragraphs are preceded by a blank line, none of them should be indented.

Footnotes, references

As a reader, I dislike footnotes. If in mid-page I shift my attention to the foot of the page, I seldom find the result worth the interruption. If I do not, I wonder but never know what I have missed.

Geoffrey Vickers, *Freedom in a Rocking Boat*

This quotation illustrates the first rule of footnotes: avoid them if possible. However, if you do need footnotes, this is how to handle them.

Footnotes can go at the bottom of the page or at the

end of the essay or report (in which case they are called endnotes). The latter is much the easier way of dealing with them unless you are using a word-processor that can handle footnotes automatically.

Footnotes are nowadays indicated by superscript numbers or, if that is not possible, numbers in square brackets:

. . . the Western economic system.[2]
. . . the Western economic system.[2]

Notice that footnote numbers follow punctuation marks.

The footnote itself would have the following form:

[2] *This has been noted by Smith in his study of . . .*

or:

2. This has been noted by Smith in his study of . . .

In the past, various symbols were used to cross-refer to footnotes: * † ‡. Do not use these; use numbers. However, if you have no more than one footnote per page, and the footnotes appear at the foot of the relevant pages rather than as endnotes at the end of the text, then it is acceptable to use asterisks:

. . . the Western economic system. *
* *This has been noted by Smith in his study of . . .*

If there are footnotes at the bottom of a page, there must a line between them and the text of the page.

References and bibliography

The best current method of giving references to other works is the following:

. . . *the Western economic system (Landon 2003: 35–53)*.

Here you give the surname of the person you are referring to and the year of the publication, which together direct the reader to a publication listed in your bibliography. There then follows a colon, and the numbers of the particular pages of the publication that you are referring the reader to.

If you refer to the author of the publication within the flow of a sentence, the style of the cross-reference is slightly different:

. . . *the Western economic system, as Landon (2003: 38) notes*.

Books are listed in a bibliography by the surname of the author, then the year of the publication:

Landon, L (2003) *The Economics of Western Aid* Edinburgh: Daimen Books

Note that the year of publication is in round brackets, the title in italics and the place of publication and the publisher in non-italic letters, separated by a colon. Other styles are acceptable; a slightly different one is used in the bibliography of this book (see page 278). Look at the bibliography styles in books you use and copy whichever suits you.

A colon is used when you are giving the title of a book that also has a subtitle:

Leech, G N (1981) *Semantics: The Study of Meaning* Harmondsworth: Penguin.

Book and journal titles are written in italic (or underlined in handwritten texts), whereas articles in journals or chapters of books are given in non-italic print, within quotation marks:

Selham, J (1990) 'I Love the Sound of Breaking Glass' *Demolition Monthly* 31: 23–27

Another method of giving references to other works is the 'numbered note' system in which other works being quoted or referred to are indicated by numbers in square brackets:

. . . *the Western economic system [14].*

Although references in this system are shorter and therefore less intrusive to your main text, they are less informative than the 'author and date' system, in that they give no indication of the author and generally do not include page references to the text being quoted. Compare the following:

. . . *the Western economic system (Landon 2003: 35–53).*
. . . *the Western economic system [14].*

If you use the 'numbered note' system, sources are listed in your bibliography by the relevant numbers, but the rest of the reference is the same as in the 'author and date' system:

[14] Landon, L (2003) *The Economics of Western Aid* Edinburgh: Daimen Books

Quotations

Short quotations integrated into a sentence should be marked off by quotation marks:

As Drummond says, 'the history of this population movement is unknown to us, because the records of the kingdom for this period have not yet been found'.

The quotation may be preceded by a comma or a colon:

As George Mikes once said, 'An Englishman, even if he is alone, forms an orderly queue of one.'
As Shakespeare said: 'All the world's a stage.'

Longer quotations should begin on a new line, with a blank line above it, and should not be in quotation marks:

As Drummond says in The Hurrians*:*
The details of this population movement are unknown to us, because the records of the kingdom at that time have not yet been found. But in the following century, the influence of Hurrian culture is very marked.

A quotation that is a complete sentence should begin with a capital letter:

As George Mikes once said, 'An Englishman, even if he is alone, forms an orderly queue of one.'
As Shakespeare said: 'All the world's a stage.'

The punctuation of the quotation is in this case included within the quotation marks, and there is no full stop after the closing quotation mark.

If the full-sentence quotation is linked into the larger

sentence by a word such as 'that', you may replace the initial capital letter with a lower-case letter:

Drummond says that 'the history of this population movement is unknown to us, because the records of the kingdom for this period have not yet been found'.

Some authorities, however, prefer that the initial capital letter be retained:

Drummond says that 'The history of this population movement is unknown to us, because the records of the kingdom for this period have not yet been found'.

In either case, there is strictly only one sentence, and the full stop at the end of the sentence goes *outside* the closing quotation mark.
• If you wish to shorten a quotation when you quote it by omitting one or more words, you show the omission by means of ellipsis points:

The details of this population movement are unknown to us, . . . But in the following century the influence of Hurrian culture is very marked.

Any punctuation mark that occurs before an ellipsis, whether within or at the end of a sentence, should be retained:

There is no science that is not capable of additions; . . . If this be true of all other sciences, why not of morals? . . . The very conception of this as possible is in the highest degree encouraging.

William Godwin, *Enquiry Concerning Political Justice*

When an ellipsis indicates an uncompleted sentence, it should not be followed by a full stop. An ellipsis can, of course, be followed by a question mark or an exclamation mark:

Ah, yes. You're Jones. And your job is to . . . ?

• Alterations or additions to a quotation should be in square brackets:

The details of this population movement [as seen by those who took part in it] are unknown to us, because the records of the kingdom at that time have not yet been found. But in the following century, the influence of Hurrian culture is very marked.

If you notice that something is incorrect in a quotation, you should leave the error as it is but indicate that you have noticed it by means of the word 'sic' in square brackets ('sic' is Latin for 'thus'):

But in the following century, the influence of Hurian [sic] culture is very marked.

If there is something you think may be wrong, you may indicate this by a question mark in square brackets:

The battle took place in 1137[?] BC.

Technical terms

Adjective
An **adjective** is a word that describes something:

*a **big** dog*
*a **green** car*

An **adjective phrase** is a phrase containing an adjective:

*a **very big** dog*

Adverb
An **adverb** is a word that adds information about the action of a verb:

*They all laughed **loudly**.*
*I'll be back **tonight**.*

An **adverbial phrase** is a phrase that functions like an adverb:

*I'll be back **a week on Tuesday**.*

Apposition
Two nouns or noun phrases are said to be **in apposition** when they denote the same person or thing and have the same function in the sentence:

***My brother Philip** lives in **Canberra, the capital of Australia**.*

Article
The **articles** are the words *a, an* and *the*.

Clause
A **clause** is a sentence that forms part of a larger sentence. There are two types of clause: **main clauses** and **subordinate clauses**. A main clause is the chief clause of a sentence:

Anne jumped when the phone rang.

Subordinate clauses function like adverbs, for example saying when or why something happens:

*Anne jumped **when the phone rang**.*
*I'm crying **because I'm happy**.*
*I'll come **if I can**.*

Main clauses may be linked by words such as *and* and *but*:

Anne jumped and the dog barked when the phone rang.

Complement
A **complement** is a word or phrase that says something about the subject or the object in a sentence:

*The car is **red**.*
*They painted the car **red**.*
*Simon is **a lawyer**.*

Conjunction

A conjunction is a word that links clauses:

*I'll come **when** I'm ready.*
*Finish that **before** you leave.*
*We tried **and** tried **but** we couldn't open the box.*

Infinitive

An infinitive is the form of a verb that goes with the word 'to':

*I want **to leave** now.*

Sometimes an infinitive is not preceded by 'to':

*You can **go** now.*

Lower-case and upper-case

A **lower-case** letter is an ordinary small letter. An **upper-case** letter is a capital letter.

Noun

A **noun** is a word that names a person or thing:

*The **dog** barked loudly.*
*The **boys** were playing in the **garden**.*
*You must always tell the **truth**.*

A **noun phrase** is a phrase that contains a noun and one or more adjectives:

*The **big black dog** barked loudly.*

Object

The **object** of a verb is the person or thing that receives the action of the verb:

*She was reading **a book**.*
*Pay **the money** and let's go.*

Participle

A **participle** is a form of a verb that ends in *-ing*, *-ed*, *-en*, etc:

***Running** to catch the bus, I tripped and fell.*
***Protected** by a wall 17 metres thick, the town has survived many onslaughts.*
***Hidden** by the trees, we watched what was happening.*

Phrase

A phrase is a group of two or more words that have the same function in a sentence as a single word. Compare:

*I like **dogs**.*	*I like **big dogs**.*
*He ran **quickly**.*	*He ran **very quickly**.*

Predicate

The predicate is everything in a clause except the subject:

*She **cut off her hair in front of the bathroom mirror**.*

Preposition

A preposition is a word or phrase that shows the relationship between a noun or noun phrase and the rest of the sentence:

*Hidden **by** the trees, we watched what was happening.*
*My brother Philip lives **in** Canberra, the capital **of** Australia.*
*She cut off her hair **in front of** the mirror.*

Pronoun
A pronoun is a word such as *he, she, I, we*, etc.

Question
A **direct question** is a question in the form in which it is actually spoken:

Where are they?

An **indirect question** is a question in the form in which it is reported:

*He asked **where they were**.*

A **question tag** is a short question added to the end of a sentence:

*You're coming too, **aren't you**?*

Relative clause
A **defining relative clause** picks out a particular person or thing:

*What's the name of that song **you keep singing**?*

A **non-defining relative clause** provides extra information about something:

*The lyrics of the song, **which she wrote five years ago**, are based on an experience she had at school.*

Sentence

A **simple sentence** is a group of words in which there is (usually) a subject and a verb:

She heard footsteps outside.

A **composite sentence** is a sentence consisting of two or more clauses:

She heard footsteps outside but she couldn't see anyone.
She heard footsteps outside but when she opened the door there was no-one there.

Verb

A **verb** is a word that describes an action:

*The boys **swam** ashore.*
*The children **were stroking** the rabbit.*

A verb may simply link a subject and a complement:

*The rabbit **was** brown and white.*

Bibliography

Allen, R E *One Step Ahead: Punctuation* Oxford: Oxford University Press, 2002

Carey, G V *Mind the Stop: A Brief Guide to Punctuation with a Note on Proof-Correction* Harmondsworth: Penguin Books, 1971 (first published by Cambridge University Press, 1939)

Cook, C K *Line by Line: How to Improve Your Own Writing* Boston: Houghton Mifflin, 1985

Daniel, E *The Grammar, History, and Derivation of the English Language* (2nd Edition) London: National Society's Depository, 1883

Davidson, G *Chambers Guide to Grammar and Usage* Edinburgh: Chambers, 1996

Fowler, H W *A Dictionary of Modern English Usage* Oxford: Clarendon Press, 1926

Fowler, H W and Fowler, F G *The King's English* Oxford: Clarendon Press, 1906

Gowers, Sir E *Plain Words: A Guide to the Use of English* London: His Majesty's Stationery Office, 1948

Jarvie, G *Good Punctuation Guide* Edinburgh: Chambers Harrap, 1992

King, G. *Good Punctuation* Glasgow: HarperCollins, 2004

McArthur, T (ed.) *The Oxford Companion to the English Language* Oxford: Oxford University Press, 1992

Nash, W *English Usage: A Guide to First Principles* London: Routledge and Kegan Paul, 1986

Partridge, E *You Have a Point There: A Guide to Punctuation and Its Allies* London: Hamish Hamilton, 1953

Readers Digest *How to Write and Speak Better* Sydney: Reader's Digest (Australia) Pty Ltd, 2nd edition 1994

Seaton, A *Focus on Grammar* Singapore: Learners Publishing (forthcoming)

Todd, L *The Cassell Guide to Punctuation* London: Cassell, 1995

Trask, R L *The Penguin Guide to Punctuation* London: Penguin Books, 1997

Truss, L *Eats, Shoots and Leaves* London: Profile Books, 2003

Wood, F W *Current English Usage: A Concise Dictionary* London: Macmillan, 1963

Index

abbreviations
  with capital letters 244
  of days of the week and
      months 49
  with full stops 48
  of honours 52
  including numbers 49
  Internet and texting 53
  of Latin words 52
  of names 50
  with obliques 198
  plural 49, 204
  of units of measurement 51
  of university degrees 52
AD 248
additional information
      enclosed in parentheses
      187
add-ons separated off by
      commas 93
addresses 261
adjective 272
  adjectives separated or not
      separated by commas 110,
      112
adverb 27, 272
adverbial phrase 27, 272
  also preceded by semicolon
      86, 135
alternatives
  enclosed in parentheses 187

  punctuated with obliques
      196
  separated by commas 100
American punctuation 46, 126,
      139, 152, 153, 156, 182
'and' test for commas 81, 106,
      112, 113
angle brackets 184
apostrophe 199
  differentiating between
      singular and plural
      nouns 10
  in foreign languages 207
  greengrocer's 202
  keyboarding problems 207
  for omitted letter or letters
      205
  in plural nouns 202, 207
apposition 272
  punctuation of 104
Arabic 207
article 273
asterisks replacing letters 166
backslash 196
balanced sentences
  punctuated with commas
      116
  punctuated with semicolon
      or colon? 136, 150
BC 248
bibliographies 267

boldface type for highlighting and emphasis 256

brackets 184

within brackets 189

see also parentheses

brand names, capital letters in 239

capital letters 231

in abbreviations and symbols 244

after colon in American English 152

beginning quotations 232

beginning sentences 231

for emphasis 246

in German nouns 247

in headlines 246

in letters 246

in names 234

in personification 238

in poetry 70, 233, 238

in pronouns 248

captions

exclamation marks in 74

question marks in 63

without full stops 47

chapter and verse references, colons in 153

Chinese 207

clause 30, 273

main clause 30, 78, 79, 81, 83, 84, 90

subordinate clause 30, 79, 81, 83, 101

clock times, colons in 153

colon 140

before quotations 149

in chapter and verse references 153

in clock times 153

followed by dash 146

introducing definitions 144

introducing examples 153

introducing explanations, descriptions and expansions 140, 144

introducing lists 145

introducing subtitles and subheadings 151

introducing summing-up 148

in memos 154

in ratios 153

showing close link between statements 138, 143

in time expressions 55

colon, comma or dash preceding explanations? 97

colon or comma before direct speech? 149

colon or dash introducing lists? 162

colon or semicolon in balanced or contrasting sentences? 136, 150

colon or semicolon introducing lists? 137, 147

comma

affecting meaning 8

in American punctuation 182

in balanced sentences 116

comma – *cont.*
  basic principles of use 78,
    80, 86
  beside parentheses and
    quotation marks 125
  between main clauses 84
  between series of words or
    phrases 105
  between subject and verb 79
  in co-ordinated phrases 105
  in direct speech 126
  introducing expansions and
    explanations 142–3
  making difference in
    meaning 96
  marking pauses 97
  needed between adjectives?
    110, 112, 114
  not between adjectives
    forming a unit of
    meaning 110
  in numbers 128
  obeying sentence structure
    or rhythm? 120
  Oxford comma 107
  replaced by semicolon for
    clarity 118, 134
  replacing full stop in direct
    speech 44
  separating main clauses
    without conjunctions 90
  separating subordinate
    clause and main clause
    81, 83
  serial comma 107
  showing difference in
    meaning 114
  when to omit 78
comma, colon or dash
    preceding explanations?
    97
comma or colon before direct
    speech 149
comma or semicolon? 86, 91,
    133, 136
command ending with full stop
    or exclamation mark? 43
commas, parentheses or
    dashes? 96, 158, 186
comments
  enclosed in parentheses 184
  punctuated by dashes 157
  in square brackets 188
complement 27, 273
'complete thought' test for
    sentences 25
composite sentence 29, 277
  punctuation of 32, 78, 79,
    81, 83, 84
conjunction 30, 274
consequence indicated by
    colon 138, 143
consequently preceded by
    semicolon 86, 135
contrast
  punctuated by comma or
    semicolon? 91
  punctuated by semicolon or
    colon? 136
correspondence 261
curly brackets 184
dash 155
  in American punctuation
    156

dash – *cont.*
  for emphasis 158
  following a colon 146
  indicating an incomplete
    sentence 160
  indicating a range 164
  introducing a definition 163
  introducing a summing-up
    148, 163
  linking dash 156, 164
  long dash 166
  marking a pause or
    hesitation 162, 194
  with repeated words 163
  separating dash 156, 157
dash, comma or colon in
  explanations? 97
dash or colon introducing
  lists? 162
dash or ellipsis points ending
  incomplete sentence? 162,
  193
dash or hyphen ? 156
dashes, parentheses or
  commas? 96, 158, 186
dashes round comments and
  interruptions 157, 160
dates 197, 262
days of the week, abbreviations
  of 49
decimal currency 54
decimal numbers 54
defining relative clause 101,
  276
  punctuation of 101
definition introduced by
  colon 144

introduced by dash 163
description preceded by colon
  140, 144
differences in meaning
  indicated by hyphens 210
direct question 276
direct speech 257
  capital letters in 232
  comma replacing full stop
    in 44
  commas in 44, 126
  punctuation of 177, 257
ellipsis 191
ellipsis points
  ending uncompleted
    sentence 193
  indicating omission 191
  indicating a pause or
    hesitation 194
  as link within a sentence 195
ellipsis points or dash ending
  uncompleted sentence?
  193
email 262
  abbreviations 53
  exclamation marks in 74
  full stops in email addresses
  55
emphasis
  indicated by a dash 158
  indicated by an exclamation
    mark 76
  indicated by boldface type
    256
  indicated by capital letters
    246
  indicated by italics 253

emphasis – *cont.*
  indicated by quotation
    marks 174
  pause for emphasis marked
    by comma 99
endnotes 266
essays 262
examples preceded by colon 153
exclamation in question form
  72
exclamation mark 68
  in email greetings 74
  for emphasis 76
  in headlines, captions, titles,
    etc 74
  indicating humour 74
  indicating scorn 76
  indicating surprise 75
  in mid-sentence 70
  multiple exclamation marks
    66, 72
  in poetry 69
  position of beside quotation
    marks and parentheses
    71
exclamation mark or full stop
  with commands? 43, 69
expansion or explanation
  introduced by colon 140
  introduced by comma 142
fine-tooth comb 225
footnotes 265
for example preceded by
  semicolon 86, 135
foreign words
  apostrophes in 207
  capital letters in 247

  in italic 254
forward slash 196
fractions
  hyphens in 216
  obliques in 198
fragment (sentence) 36
  used for emphasis 38
fronting 91
full stop 42
  in abbreviations 48
  in American punctuation
    182
  at end of request 43
  at end of sentence 42
  omission of 46, 65, 73
  position of beside
    parentheses and
    quotation marks 45
  replaced by comma in direct
    speech 44
full stop or colon? 55, 130
full stop or exclamation mark
  with commands? 43
full stop or semicolon? 87
furthermore preceded by
  semicolon 86, 135
German nouns, capital letters
  in 247
greengrocer's apostrophe in
  plural nouns 202
headings in essays and reports
  264
headlines
  capital letters in 246
  exclamation marks in 74
  no full stop at end of 47
  question marks in 63

hence preceded by semicolon 86

hesitation marked by ellipsis points or dash 162, 194

highlighting
with boldface type 256
with italics 253
with quotation marks 173

honours, abbreviation of 52

how phrases 92

however
preceded by semicolon 86, 88, 135
separated off by commas 89

humour indicated by exclamation marks 74

hyphen 209
in adverb + adjective phrases 212
for clarity 215
differentiating words 9
in fractions 216
indicating stammering or slow speech 229
loss of 226
in multi-word nouns 215
in numbers 216
in phrases before nouns 210
with prefixes, suffixes and word-forming elements 220
presence or absence of a hyphen affecting meaning 9, 210
splitting words at end of line 227
in two-word phrases 216

hyphen or dash? 156

ID or *I.D.*? 53

incomplete sentences punctuated by dash or ellipsis points? 160, 162

indirect question 276
not ending with a question mark 57

indirect speech, no quotation marks in 169

infinitive 28, 32, 274

instead preceded by semicolon 86, 135

intention governing punctuation 60, 72

Internet abbreviations 53

interruption
enclosed in parentheses 184
punctuated with commas 93
punctuated with dashes 157, 160

-isms: capital letters with? 238

italics 252
for emphasis 253
for foreign words and phrases 254
for highlighting 253
in titles and names 255

keyboarding apostrophes 207

Latin words, abbreviations of 52

letters (alphabetical) and numbers in lists with brackets 187

letters (alphabetical), plurals written with apostrophes 204

letters (correspondence) 261
  capital letters in 246
linking dash 156, 164
linking with obliques 196
list
  preceded by dash or colon?
    145, 162
  preceded by colon or
    semicolon? 137, 147
long dash 166
main clause 30
  separated by comma? 84, 90
  separated from subordinate
    clause by comma? 79, 81,
    83
m-dash 155
meaning, punctuation
  governed by 60, 72
memos, colons in 154
months, abbreviations of 49
moreover preceded by
  semicolon 86, 135
m-rule 155
MS or *M.S.*? 53
names
  abbreviations of 50
  capital letters in 234
  capital letters in words
    derived from 238
n-dash 155
nevertheless preceded by
  semicolon 86, 135
nicknames enclosed by
  quotation marks 175
no one or *no-one*? 225
non-defining relative clause
  102, 276

  punctuation of 102
noun 274
noun phrase 274
nouns requiring hyphens 215,
  217
n-rule 155
numbers
  abbreviations containing 49
  commas in 128
  hyphens in 216
  plurals written with
    apostrophes 205
numbers and letters in lists
  with brackets 187
object 27, 275
oblique 196
  in abbreviations 198
  in dates 197
  in fractions 198
  as links between words 196
  marking alternatives 196
  in periods of time 197
  in quoting poetry 198
  in ratios 197
  in website addresses 198
omissions
  marked by apostrophes 205
  marked by asterisks 166
  marked by commas 117
  marked by long dashes 166
Oxford comma 107
paragraph 250, 265
parentheses 184
  position of comma beside
    125
  position of exclamation
    mark beside 71

parentheses – *cont.*
  position of full stop beside 45
  position of question mark
    beside 64
  question mark in
    parentheses indicating
    uncertainty 67
  round alternatives 187
  round interruptions,
    comments and additional
    information 185, 187
  round numbers and letters
    in lists 187
parentheses, commas or
  dashes? 96, 158, 186
participle 32, 275
pause 97
  for emphasis 99
  marked by comma 97
  marked by dash 162
  marked by ellipsis points or
    dash 194
pause test for commas 80, 93,
  97, 100, 113
pause vs structure governing
  comma placement 120
period *see* full stop
personification requiring a
  capital letter 238
phrasal verb 218
  hyphens in adjectives
    formed from 220
  hyphens in nouns formed
    from 219
phrase 275
plural nouns with apostrophes
  202, 207

poetry
  capital letters or lower-case
    letters in 23, 70
  exclamation marks in 69
possession marked by an
  apostrophe 199
postcode 51
predicate 26, 275
prefixes, hyphens with 220, 221
preposition 275
pronoun 276
  requiring capital letter 248
PS or *P.S.*? 53
punctuation
  art, not science 15
  British and American 21, 46,
    126, 139, 152, 153, 156, 182
  choosing an appropriate
    level 16
  clarifying the structure and
    meaning of a text 4, 5
  of composite sentence 32
  differentiating words 9
  good punctuation 13
  heavy and light 4, 16
  history of punctuation 3
  improving your
    punctuation 17
  linking words 8
  marking the rhythm of
    speech 4
  in the Middle Ages 4
  personal choice and taste
    13–15
  purpose of punctuation 1
  representing emotion and
    attitude 11

punctuation – *cont.*
  rules 13–15
  representing visual and
    vocal aspects of speech 2
  separating and grouping
    words 6
  use of computer
    punctuation checker 21
punctuation marks
  multiple 66, 72
  position of beside quotation
    marks 45, 64, 71, 125, 169
question 276
  ending in question mark 56
  exclamation in question
    form 60
  in the form of a statement
    43, 57
  indicating surprise 59
  part questions 60
  as request 59
  within a statement 62
question mark
  at end of sentence 56
  in headlines, captions, etc 63
  indicating uncertainty 67
  multiple 66
  not at end of indirect
    question 57
  omission of 65
  position of beside quotation
    marks, parentheses and
    dashes 64
quotation 171, 269
  beginning with capital letter
    232
  introduced by colon 149

  punctuation of 177
  showing an omission in 191
quotation marks 168
  in direct speech 169
  double and single 168
  for emphasis 174
  for highlighting 173
  indicating disagreement 174
  omission of 170
  position of comma beside
    125
  position of exclamation
    mark 71
  position of full stop beside 45
  position of question mark
    beside 64
  repetition of 171
  representing nuances of
    meaning 11
  round nicknames 175
  round titles and names 176
  single and double 168
  with other punctuation
    marks 45, 64, 71, 125, 169
ranges
  punctuated with dashes 164
  punctuated with obliques
    197
ratios
  colons in 153
  punctuated with obliques
    197
reduced sentence 34
references to footnotes, etc
  267
referring back 163
relative clause 101, 276

repeated words, usc of dash
    with 163
reports 262
request
    full stop at end of 43
    in form of question 43, 59
round brackets *see* parentheses
scientific names 256
scorn indicated by exclamation
    marks 76
semicolon 130
    replacing comma for clarity
    118, 134
semicolon or colon in
    balanced or contrasting
    sentences? 136, 150
semicolon or colon
    introducing lists? 137, 147
semicolon or comma in
    balanced sentences? 133,
    136
semicolon or comma to
    separate contrasting
    clauses? 91
semicolon or comma with
    linking words? 86
semicolon or full stop? 87, 130
sense, punctuation governed
    by 60, 72
sentence
    beginning with capital letter
    231
    composite sentence 29
    definitions of 24, 277
    fragment 36
    fragments used for
    emphasis 38

needed for good
    punctuation 23
non-sentence 36
part sentences linked by
    ellipsis points 195
recognizing sentences by
    their structure 25
reduced sentence 34
simple sentence 26
string 36
super-sentence 33, 131
separating dash 156
serial comma 107
sic 189, 271
simple sentence 26, 277
    expansion of 28
    punctuation of 29, 78
slash 196
slow speech marked by
    hyphens 229
solidus 196
speech different from writing 2
square brackets 184, 188
    round comments and
    additions 188
    round editor's queries 67
stammering indicated by
    hyphens 229
statement as question 43, 57
string (sentence) 36
structure vs pauses for comma
    placement 120
style, good viii
subject 26
subject and verb separated by
    comma 79
subordinate clause 30

separated from main clause
by comma? 79, 81, 83
subtitles and subheadings
introduced by colon 151
suffixes, hyphens with 220, 223
Sumer 3
summing-up
preceded by a colon or dash
163
preceded by a comma 103
super-sentence 33
punctuation of 33, 90, 131,
135
surprise 75
indicated by exclamation
mark 75
indicated by a question 59
symbols, capital letters with
244
TB or *T.B.*? 53
texting abbreviations 53
therefore preceded by
semicolon 86, 135
thus preceded by semicolon
86, 135
time, full stops or colons in 55
time periods linked by
obliques 197
titles
capital letters in 241, 242
exclamation marks in 74

no full stops in 47
question marks in 63
titles and names
enclosed in quotation
marks 176
in italics 255
marked by underlining 176
titles of essays and reports 262
TV or *T.V.*? 53
uncertainty marked by
question mark 67
uncompleted sentence ending
in dash or ellipsis points?
193
underlining 176, 256
units of measurement,
abbreviations of 51
university degrees 52
verb 26, 277
website addresses 55
when phrases 92
where phrases 92
wild-goose chase 225
word-forming elements,
hyphens with 220, 223
word-splitting hyphens 227
writing
development from drawing
3
different from speech 2
ZIP code 51